BRAVE BLACK WOMEN

BRAVE
BLACK WOMEN

FROM SLAVERY TO THE
SPACE SHUTTLE

Ruthe Winegarten and Sharon Kahn

UNIVERSITY OF TEXAS PRESS
AUSTIN

First edition, 1997

This book is adapted for young readers from Ruthe Winegarten's *Black Texas Women: 150 Years of Trial and Triumph* (Austin: University of Texas Press, 1995).

Requests for permission to reproduce material from this work should be sent to Permissions, University of Texas Press, Box 7819, Austin, TX 78713-7819.

(∞) The paper used in this publication meets the minimum requirements of American National Standard for Information Sciences — Permanence of Paper for Printed Library Materials, ANSI Z39.48-1984.

Library of Congress Cataloging-in-Publication Data
Winegarten, Ruthe.
    Brave Black women : from slavery to the space shuttle / Ruthe Winegarten and Sharon Kahn. — 1st ed.
        p.   cm.
    Adaptation of: Black Texas women. 1995.
    Includes bibliographical references and index.
    ISBN 0-292-79106-2 (alk. paper). — ISBN 0-292-79107-0 (pbk. : alk. paper)
    1. Afro-American women—Texas—History—Juvenile literature.
    2. Texas—History—1846-1950—Juvenile literature. 3. Texas—History—
    1951- —Juvenile literature. [1. Afro-Americans—Texas—History.
    2. Women—Texas—History. 3. Texas—History.] I. Kahn, Sharon, 1934- .
    II. Winegarten, Ruthe. Black Texas Women. III. Title.
    E185.93.T4B563 1997
    305.48´960730764—dc20
                                                                96-35614
                                                                    AC

Design by Elizabeth Towler Menon

Cover photos, *clockwise from top right:* Mae Jemison (NASA); Ethelyn Taylor Chisum (Texas/Dallas History Archives Division, Dallas Public Library); Anne Lundy (photo by Jeff St. Mary, courtesy Anne Lundy); Barbara Jordan (*Houston Chronicle*); Bessie Coleman (Smithsonian Institution); Phylicia Rashad (Adept New American Museum, Mount Vernon, N.Y.); chopping cotton (photo by Dorothea Lange, Photographs and Prints Division, Schomburg Center for Research in Black Culture, The New York Public Library, Astor, Lenox and Tilden Foundations). *Center:* Carlette Guidry (copyright Susan Allen Camp, Women's Athletics Division, University of Texas at Austin).

Contents

Preface

vii

Acknowledgments

ix

1 Slavery : Overcoming Fear

1

2 Freed Women : How They Survived

13

3 Education : The Road to a Better Life

25

4 Community Building : Women United!

37

5 Fighting Oppression : For the Vote and Against Violence

47

6 Work : Women of Achievement

59

7 World War II : Serving Their Country
73

8 The Civil Rights Movement : Equal Justice for All
81

9 The Arts and Sports : Creating and Performing
95

10 Law and Politics : Women of Power
113

11 Barbara Jordan : Defender of the Constitution
127

Barbara Jordan Chronology
149

Sources of Quotations by Barbara Jordan
152

Reading List
155

Credits
157

Index
161

Preface

I won't know what the next step is until I get there. I know that when I went to Boston, and Austin, and Washington, I took with me everything I had learned before. And that's what I will do this time. That's the point of it, isn't it? To bring everything you have with you wherever you go.

BARBARA JORDAN spoke these words to students—her favorite audience. Though she was a legislator, an orator, and a great American leader, her role as teacher was the most important one, and she taught us all. Barbara Jordan died as this book was being written, and it is her spirit which breathes life into its chapters.

Barbara Jordan told us in the words above that the point of life is to bring everything you have with you wherever you go. Though she was a child of the twentieth century, she brought with her the rich heritage of all the brave black women who had gone before her and who worked alongside her. As she succeeded in the world, she took with her everything she had learned before. What she brought with her is what this book is all about.

The great poet W. B. Yeats wrote:

O chestnut-tree, great rooted blossomer,
Are you the leaf, the blossom or the bole?
O body swayed to music, O brightening glance,
How can we know the dancer from the dance?

("Among School Children," 1928)

Like the chestnut tree, Barbara Jordan sprang from the great roots of African American women who nourished this country for three centuries through slavery to freedom. She is a part of them, and they of her. *Brave Black Women* tells us their stories and shows us their photographs, emphasizing the black women of Jordan's home state of Texas, whose legacy she inherited. Many of them, along with Jordan, achieved national fame.

Barbara Jordan said, "I get from the soil and spirit of Texas the feeling that I, as an individual, can accomplish whatever I want to, and that there are no limits, that you can just keep going, keep soaring. I like that spirit."

Dignity marks these lives with a graceful step, uniting Barbara Jordan and those who came before her. Join us as we follow, in pictures and words, the dancer and the dance.

Ruthe Winegarten and Sharon Kahn, 1996

Acknowledgments

We are grateful for the excellent editorial assistance of Dr. Dorothea Brown, Dr. Nancy Baker Jones, and Frieda Werden.

We thank our family members for their love and support: David, Suzanne, and Jon Weizenbaum and Nancy Nussbaum; and Debbie Winegarten, Marc Sanders, and Martha Wilson.

Our editor at U.T. Press, Theresa J. May, believed in the value of this book and has lent constant encouragement, for which we are most appreciative.

CHAPTER 1

Slavery:
Overcoming Fear

As you listen to these words of Abraham Lincoln, relate them to the concept of a national community in which every last one of us participates: "As I would not be a slave, so I would not be a master. This expresses my idea of a democracy."

BARBARA JORDAN

Slave women worked without pay. Former slave Mariah Carr of Marshall demonstrates the spinning wheel. During the Civil War, she spun thread for long hours to make clothes for the Confederate soldiers.

WHAT WAS SLAVERY LIKE?

BRAVE black women endured years of slavery until the end of the Civil War. Their own lives, and those of their families, belonged to the slave owners. These masters and mistresses controlled their slaves' actions during the workday.

Even at night and on the weekends, slave women often worked, washing, ironing, spinning thread, and sewing. Despite many hardships, slaves remembered and continued their African traditions, where women were honored and respected as they grew older and wiser.

Have you ever picked up a big dog weighing fifty pounds? Was the load so heavy you almost dropped it? Slave children worked in the fields picking cotton. The sacks they filled could hold as much as fifty pounds. Some women picked three hundred or sometimes four hundred pounds of cotton a day, as much as the men. The children worked beside them, filling sacks made in a smaller size. They had to work fast and keep picking, even when they were hot, tired, and sleepy. Sometimes they were hungry and thirsty, too, and frightened of the overseer, the slaves' boss. They didn't have much time to play. Children as young as five or six also baby-sat for infants and toddlers, gathered firewood, swept the yard, and tended animals.

*"Chopping cotton" means hoeing to get the weeds out.
Slave women and sharecroppers worked hard in the cotton fields
from sunup to sundown. They planted, chopped, or picked
depending on the season.*

Clara Anderson was six years old when she and a girl friend were captured by a white man. It was Christmas Day, 1843. They were stolen from their parents in Maryland and brought to Texas as slaves. Clara was badly mistreated. Years later, she remembered her many troubles:

"This all happened in Austin, Texas. The folks would give me a little to eat, and half the time I was almost starved to death. There was some little Jewish children who lived nearby, and every day when they would come from school, they'd leave me some food. They'd hide this food in a tree-stump, where I'd go and git it. Those children would bring me buttered bread, cakes, and other things."

Clara Anderson was six years old when she was captured in Maryland and brought to Austin as a slave.

Clara Anderson lived to be freed after the Civil War and to raise her own family. She said, "I always had to work, and to this day, I barely know my A-B-C's." But Clara had a good mind. She remembered her life as a slave and told her stories instead of writing them down. The stories are part of a collection of slave tales that will be preserved for generations to come.

Katie Darling's master and mistress had six children. She nursed all of them. She said, "I stayed in the house with them and slept on a pallet on the floor, and as soon as I was big enough to tote the milk pail they put me to milking, too. Massa had more than 100 cows, and most of the time me and Violet did all the milking. We'd better be in that cowpen by five o'clock [in the morning]. One morning massa caught me letting one of the calves do some milking, and he let me off without whipping that time, but that didn't mean he was always good, because those cows had more feeling for us than massa and missy."

Hannah Mullins was born a slave. She and her family lived in a double log cabin with two rooms separated by a hall. A big bell rang in the morning for the slaves to get up very early, and again at bedtime. Hannah was raised in the slave nursery with other slave children until she was five years old. At mealtime, the cooks set two long wooden troughs on the table and filled them with crumbled corn bread and milk. Hannah and the other children lined up on each side of the table with their wooden spoons. When the women in charge of the nursery told the children to begin eating, they all dug in at once. Each one raced to fill up before the food was gone. Even then, they were still hungry the rest of the day.

CHILDREN WERE SOLD, TOO

MEMBERS of many slave families were separated from each other. Mintie Maria Miller remembered a heartbreaking experience:

> "When I was little, my brother, uncle, aunt and mother was sold and I went with 'em. My father wasn't sold so he couldn't go. My sister got on de wagon to go, too, and de marster said, 'Adeline, you can't come. You got to stay here with Mistress.' Dat's de last I ever seen my sister. She was four years old."

Slaves who ran away were often hunted down with dogs, and their owners placed ads in the newspapers for their return. One man offered to pay a $20 reward for the return of "Eliza, a little negro girl about 8 or nine years old." A slave named Rhodie discovered a successful recipe for "keeping the hounds from following you . . . take black pepper and put it in your socks and run without your shoes. It made the hounds sneeze."

KIAN LONG, A TEXAS PIONEER

KIAN LONG was the slave and lifelong companion of Jane Long, one of the first white women to settle in Texas. Thirteen-year-old Kian and Jane spent a freezing winter alone on Bolivar Island across from Galveston in 1821 while Texas was still part of Spain. The women survived by shooting birds and catching fish, which they shared with their loyal dog. Because the women were afraid of the Karankawa Indians who lived nearby, they ran a red flannel petticoat up the flagpole and periodically fired off the cannon to give the impression that the fort was still protected by soldiers. Kian helped Jane give birth in an ice-covered tent, and later the women ran two inns. The first gunpowder of the Texas Revolution was even stored behind their inn in Brazoria. Kian was given permission to marry, and she and her husband had four children, who were slaves, too. But they were all freed after the Civil War. Kian's descendants were free. One grandson, Henry C. Breed, became a Houston police officer.

OPPOSITE: *Some black women were free before the Civil War. A few even owned slaves.*

FREE WOMEN OF COLOR

NOT all black women before the Civil War were slaves. A few hundred were free women of color. Their children were also free since they took the status of their mothers. Free people of color were not considered full citizens. They could not vote, serve on juries, or hold office. (Of course, no other women could either.) But most were hard-working and industrious members of their communities, and their neighbors respected them.

Some women were nurses, laundresses, and cooks. Others were seamstresses, boardinghouse keepers, and sellers of milk and butter.

A few free women of color, like Tamar Morgan of Brazoria, became prosperous businesswomen and property owners. She came to Texas as a slave, but she worked hard, saved her money, and bought her freedom. Her husband, Samuel H. Hardin, a barber, came to Texas with Stephen F. Austin's original "Old Three Hundred" group of colonists. Even respected people of color like Tamar and Samuel had trouble keeping their freedom. The couple asked their neighbors for help. The neighbors signed a petition asking that Tamar and Samuel be allowed to remain in Texas. It was one of the few such petitions granted by the Texas Congress. Within a few years, Tamar owned four town lots and one hundred acres of good land.

Charity Bird of Jefferson supported herself by baking cakes and selling them. She made enough money one year to take an enjoyable vacation back to the United States. (Texas was an independent republic at that time.) Fanny McFarland, a Houston laundress, saved her money, invested in property, and became quite wealthy. She was one of that city's first successful real estate owners.

OPPOSITE: *Doing the laundry was hard work.*
Monday was usually wash day.

THE YELLOW ROSE OF TEXAS

DID you know that the song "The Yellow Rose of Texas" was written about a black woman? Some African American women like Emily West (sometimes called Emily Morgan) came to Texas already free. She became the most famous of them and is sometimes known as the Yellow Rose of Texas. A native of New York, she came to Texas with Mrs. Lorenzo de Zavala in 1835. Emily was captured by General Santa Anna of Mexico on his way to fight General Sam Houston and the Texas troops. One tall Texas tale claims that right before the Battle of San Jacinto, Emily sent Houston the location of the Mexican troops. Santa Anna was so interested in courting Emily that he didn't realize Houston's forces were getting ready to attack. The Mexican Army was unprepared, and the Texans won the battle in eighteen minutes. Emily later applied for a passport, stating that she had lost her freedom papers on the San Jacinto battlefield. She is believed to have returned home to New York in 1837.

CHAPTER 2

Freed Women:
How They Survived

You have got to be able to love yourself—love yourself strongly,
and not let anybody disabuse you of your self-respect.

BARBARA JORDAN

Aᴜᴛᴇʀ the Confederate armies surrendered and the Civil War ended, slaves were declared free. Texas slaves were freed on June 19, 1865. Imagine your feelings if you had been imprisoned for a long time and suddenly were set free. What if all your relatives had been in prison, too, and none of you had a place to live, or food to eat, or money? What would you do?

When the slaves were freed, many began searching for family members who had been sold away to other owners. Women and men who had not been allowed to marry now held wedding ceremonies. And all freed slaves turned their efforts to finding ways to make a living.

LAUNDRESSES

Tʜᴇ former slave women did what they knew best and what was needed—doing the laundry—but now they got paid. There was no indoor plumbing in those days. Women and children had to carry water from a well or a river, sometimes very far away. Women spent long hours over pots of boiling water. One pot was for soapy water, and sometimes two or more were used for rinsing. The clothes had to be pushed down in the water and pulled out with big sticks. The heavy, wet clothes were wrung out by hand. Finally, the clothes were either hung on a line or laid out on bushes to dry in the sun. This was an all-day job.

*After freedom, mothers and children worked together to earn money
for their families by doing laundry for other people.*

Many slave women used to press other people's cotton clothes.
Some heavy irons used by slaves had a bell in the handle so that
when the bell stopped ringing, the mistress knew her slave had
stopped ironing. After freedom, women continued doing the laundry with heavy irons. In the days before electricity, they had several irons heating up on the fire while they ironed with the one
already hot. Annie Mae Hunt recalled, "I could iron a shirt or a
child's dress so a fly couldn't stand on the collar. A fly, he would
slip off."

Laundry was hard work, but it was a job that let a woman go
into business for herself. If she moved to a new town or a big city,

she could usually find laundry to do. She would either go to different people's houses and do the wash there, or take their dirty clothes to her own house, so she could watch her children and get them to help.

In the 1870s, steam laundries came to Texas and some women worked there instead of at home. In Galveston, laundry workers went on strike in 1877, the first time ever for Texas women. They were protesting their low pay and demanding $1.50 a day. They marched up and down the streets shouting "We will starve no more" and boarded up the shops of some steam laundry owners who refused to pay more money. We don't know whether they won the strike or not.

SHARECROPPERS

FAMILIES like Mintie Maria Miller's reunited and began to live together in family groups. They shared their meals, houses, and expenses, and helped one another to survive. These extended families enjoyed living together once again.

Even if they only had the skills of field workers, most women at first refused to go back to work in the old, slave way, with mean overseers watching them every minute. They wanted to be near their own homes. So the owners of the old plantations divided the

Many newly freed people began farming for themselves.
This family was able to buy a horse.

land into shares. Each family rented a plot of land from the owner and paid for it with part of the crop that they raised. Most women then continued working alongside their husbands in the fields as sharecroppers.

Unfortunately, most of the farm families had to borrow money from the owners for seeds and tools and fertilizer. Often they didn't make enough money to pay off their debts. The landowners usually cheated them, too, especially if they couldn't read. And brutal men would attack them if they tried to defend their rights. So sharecropping became very much like being in slavery.

JUNETEENTH

ABRAHAM LINCOLN had issued the Emancipation Proclamation freeing the slaves on January 1, 1863, but it wasn't until the Union Army beat the Confederates that freedom came. After the war was over, Union General Gordon Granger landed at Galveston, Texas, on June 19, 1865. He declared that Texas slaves were now free. Katie Darling's owners continued holding her illegally as a slave for six more years until her brother finally rescued her. She recalled how happy she was to "get away from that old devil missy."

June 19 became Emancipation Day for freed people and is

*This family dressed up to celebrate Juneteenth in Austin around
1900. Juneteenth is still celebrated every year to recall
June 19, 1865, when freedom was announced to slaves in Texas.*

known as Juneteenth. Communities in Texas still celebrate this
date, and in 1980 it became an official Texas state holiday.
Juneteenth became so famous that today it is also celebrated across
the United States. It is the nation's oldest African American holiday.

Festivities often include picnics, games, parades, and speeches.
Best of all is the food: fried chicken, barbecue, potato salad, and all
kinds of delicious desserts—lemon, pecan, and sweet potato pies,
peach cobbler, coconut and caramel layer cakes, and red soda
water.

THE CUNEY FAMILY

WHAT does freedom feel like? Many people would say that freedom means being whatever you want to be and doing whatever you want to do. The newly freed slaves also wanted to make their own decisions, but their former owners, who still had wealth and power, often tried to hold them back. Even the few slaves who had been educated found it hard to be accepted for their accomplishments.

Norris Wright Cuney was the son of a slave woman, Adeline Cuney, and a white plantation owner who freed her and their children. His parents sent him and his brothers north to study in Pittsburgh, Pennsylvania, before the Civil War. After the war, Norris Cuney used his education to become a leader of the Republican Party. He was named sergeant-at-arms of the Texas House of Representatives, was elected to the Galveston school board, and was appointed to be a federal customs collector in Galveston. He owned a prosperous stevedoring business loading and unloading ships.

In 1886, Norris condemned the lynching of five black men in Brenham. He wrote and made speeches attacking the cowardly mob act. Although he received threats, he refused to remain silent.

Norris Cuney married Adelina Dowdie, a schoolteacher. In 1886, Adelina Dowdie Cuney decided to catch a train from Galveston to Houston. Because of segregation—separation of

Maud Cuney Hare of Galveston was a noted music historian, folklorist, pianist, and playwright. She went to music school in Boston.

black people from white—the conductor locked the door to the first-class coach when he saw Mrs. Cuney coming. He did not want her to sit alongside white passengers. When his back was turned, she tricked him. She put her dainty foot on her brother-in-law's knee, and he boosted her in through a window. When the conductor entered the coach to collect tickets, he was surprised and annoyed to see Mrs. Cuney sitting there "quite contented and with perfect ease and indifference."

Adelina and Norris's daughter, Maud Cuney Hare, followed in her parents' footsteps. She was inspired by her mother's beautiful soprano voice to study music herself. In 1890, Maud enrolled in the New England Conservatory of Music in Boston. For a while, Maud and the only other black student lived in the dormitory undisturbed. Then school authorities wrote her father a letter, informing him that because of racial prejudice, they wanted him to move Maud to a home outside the school. Norris was very angry and wrote back refusing to move Maud. Maud, too, refused to move, even though some of the students continued to insult her. But she had a strong backbone and persevered.

She continued to defy segregation. When she taught at the Deaf, Dumb, and Blind Institute for Colored Youth in Austin, she was scheduled to play a recital at the Opera House. Then the managers announced that black and white audience members could not sit together. Whites could sit on the first floor, but blacks would have to sit in the balcony. Maud and her teacher canceled the concert there, and she performed at the Deaf, Dumb, and Blind Institute instead, so black citizens would not feel insulted.

Maud settled in Boston later and launched a highly successful career. She traveled around the country giving concerts and lectures, wrote a play called *Antar of Araby* about a black Arab warrior, and wrote an important book, *Negro Musicians and Their Music*. She also collected songs from Mexico and the Caribbean.

BUSINESS AND PROFESSIONAL WOMEN

BLACK women's lives on the frontier called for great strength and courage, and many found themselves doing jobs not usually performed by females. Gertrude Ross Rydolph was an excellent horsewoman on a ranch near Victoria. In 1911, she and her husband started their own ranch, where she also worked as a secretary and bookkeeper.

Other women also ran successful businesses. Jane Calloway, a Dallas widow, sold coal to keep people's houses and businesses warm. Mary A. Warren of Houston was the first black female photographer in the United States. She opened her business in 1866, right after the Civil War. A number of women became teachers, nurses, and dressmakers.

Gertrude Ross Rydolph ran a ranch near Victoria with her husband.

Mattie B. White (Mrs. Thomas J. White) moved to Austin after graduating from Walden University in Nashville, Tennessee, in 1884. She started a private school for black girls in Austin in 1892. She was also the art teacher at the state Deaf, Dumb, and Blind Institute for Colored Youth. She used sign language, written instructions, and patterns to teach students to paint, draw, embroider, knit, and weave baskets and rugs. For forty years, she didn't miss a single day of work. In her spare time, she painted bluebonnets and landscapes and did needlework.

CHAPTER 3

Education:
The Road to a Better Life

I find teaching extraordinarily satisfying.
It's a remarkable opportunity to have an impact
on the generation that will succeed me.

BARBARA JORDAN

A FTER freedom in 1865, blacks, children and grownups alike, were all eager to get an education. In the beginning most teachers, men and women, came from the North; but some Texas teachers taught the newly freed people. Teachers were both black and white.

Many parents sacrificed so their children could go to school. But tuition was expensive, and the freed slaves needed aid to provide an education for themselves and their children. Congress established the Freedmen's Bureau to help prepare the former slaves for citizenship. The bureau, assisted by northern missionary societies, opened some schools, paid part of teachers' salaries, and bought books.

CHILDREN WERE EAGER TO LEARN

UNDER slavery, most black children did not learn to read or write. But a few like Susan Merritt did. She learned the alphabet from her young mistress Bessie, who sneaked into her room at night to teach her. But when Bessie's mother, Miss Jane, found out, she hit Susan over the head with a cowhide whip, saying that black children didn't need to know anything. She threatened to whip Bessie, too. Reading could be dangerous. A child might copy an owner's signature on a pass to escape or even teach other slaves to read and write.

Freed children were eager to learn. The federal government helped start schools, but there were not enough books.

No wonder the newly freed black children were so eager to attend school and make up for lost time. Their parents organized private schools, paid teachers, and bought writing slates and beginning books, called primers. Children walked miles or rode horseback to their schools in all kinds of weather. They wanted to learn.

Clara Scales was so smart she was first in her class. She wanted to be a teacher and tried to go to school every day. But many times her daddy told her she couldn't because he needed her to "go out and chop that cotton." Maggie Matthews never went to school a day in her life, but she bought herself a blue-back speller for twenty cents and taught herself how to spell. She was proud she could outspell those who had gone to school. Mary Anne Gibson "learned fast" from her black teacher, Isabella Shaw.

TEACHING WAS NOT EASY

AT FIRST, the few former slaves who had learned to read in slavery taught the others and became schoolteachers and even principals. As years went by, other black women struggled to provide quality education for black youth, since the public schools in Texas were segregated.

From the beginning, black citizens considered education as equally important to girls and boys, women and men. Many dedicated black women taught in dusty one-room schools under poor conditions. Brave white women, often missionaries, also taught black children despite threats from other whites who feared that they could not control educated blacks. Some angry whites even burned down schoolhouses and murdered teachers. It was not easy being a teacher during these times.

THE ONE-ROOM SCHOOL

MANY schools were so small that children from kindergarten age through high school were taught in the same room with only one teacher. School supplies were always scarce in these one-room schools. When Dorothy Redus Robinson began teaching in a small South Texas town in 1929, a school trustee gave her a "zinc water bucket, a dipper, and a box of chalk." He promised to bring a load of firewood when the weather got cold, and "that was it." The school's walls had never been painted. Because the pupils did not have desks, they sat on rough wooden benches. They had no playground, no water supply, and only an outhouse for a bathroom. Mrs. Robinson had to use old textbooks, torn magazines, nuts, sticks, and even grains of corn to teach the children.

Mrs. Robinson later moved to Anderson County in East Texas, where she taught in another one-room school. She helped organize the Pine Hill PTA there. Working together, she and the parents cleared the stumps for a playground. Things gradually improved as all cooperated. She wrote a book about her experiences, *The Bell Rings at Four: A Black Teacher's Chronicle of Change.*

In rural areas, the school year was brief, often lasting only three or four months. Parents needed their children to help plant, chop, and harvest cotton. Students had to pay monthly tuition in most schools. In 1893, teachers received very low salaries, with black women teachers at the very bottom of the pay scale. In 1942, a Dallas teacher, Thelma Paige Richardson, filed suit and won equal pay for black teachers.

This teacher rode her horse to school every day in the town of Africa in Shelby County, Texas. The photograph was taken about 1924.

Many adults today appreciate all their teachers did for them. Douglas Mae Campbell Clark remembered, "Our teachers were very caring. They were like parents. We took pride in our school— it was something that bound us together."

URBAN SCHOOLS

ETHELYN TAYLOR CHISUM was a school counselor and teacher in Dallas. She spent thirty-two years as dean at Booker T. Washington High School, where she did everything from monitoring attendance to helping sick students. She made sure the principal hired a visiting nurse to keep her children healthy. Later, she was elected president of the Classroom Teachers of Dallas.

Mattie E. Durden taught in the home economics department of Anderson High School in Austin for more than thirty years. "It is something *within* that leads me on," she said, and that something gave her the courage to persist. She wanted to continue her education even after she married and had children. The president of Tillotson College in Austin was skeptical when she enrolled for the high school course. He said, "She will not be here long with two children to care for." Despite his prediction, Durden graduated as valedictorian, which meant she had the best grades in the class.

Mattie Durden's daughter, Olive Durden Brown, also went into

Ethelyn Taylor Chisum was a dean at
Booker T. Washington High School in Dallas for 32 years.

the field of education. This was a tradition of service often passed
down from mother to daughter. In the days of segregation, Olive
Brown had to leave the state to get her degree in library science—
from Hampton Institute in Virginia. She was the head librarian at
Huston-Tillotson College in Austin for thirty-three years. (Samuel
Huston College and Tillotson College were separate institutions in
the beginning. Tillotson opened in 1881 and Huston in 1900. They
merged in 1952.)

HIGHER EDUCATION

MANY of the first colleges for blacks were private schools established by religious groups. They were training young people to become teachers or ministers. Students had not always been prepared for college courses, and they had to work hard to learn basic skills like reading, writing, and arithmetic. As the colleges expanded their course offerings, students studied more difficult subjects like geometry, government, history, and science. Young women were now being trained as teachers, nurses, and home demonstration agents, and for other careers.

Tillotson was one of the first colleges for blacks in Texas. It was chartered in 1877 and opened in 1881. Female students in those years brought "one sheet, pillow, slip, dress, skirt, pair drawers, under vest, under waist, nightgown, apron, two towels, pair hose, shirtwaist, four handkerchiefs." This supply had to last them the whole year.

Many early colleges taught practical skills like cooking and sewing. Students in a cooking class at Samuel Huston College in 1902 prepared for careers in domestic service and learned how to manage their own homes.

PRAIRIE VIEW

Prairie View State Normal and Industrial Institute, which opened in 1879, was the first state-supported college for African Americans in Texas.

Student life was heavily regulated at both private and public colleges. On the Prairie View campus, "man" territory was separated from "woman" territory. These lines could not be crossed without special permission. Once, students went on strike for two days because the faculty refused to let them have a "sociable," a party with refreshments where young women and men could meet.

Young women attending Prairie View in 1899 could learn both hand and machine sewing. The machines were operated with treadles instead of electricity. The students had to learn to pump the machines with their feet while they sewed. Miss Sallie Ewell's classroom was outfitted with treadle "sewing machines, tables, charts and the necessary appliances for the proper instruction in measuring, cutting, fitting, making and mending garments and household linens."

Household Helps
• Pared apples and bananas will not darken if lemon
  juice is sprinkled on them.
• Cut flowers will keep fresh longer if slice of mild soap
  is put in water with them.
• To remove dirt from furniture, rub briskly with corn
  meal and gasoline.
• To remove fresh ink, pour on boiling water from a height.

---

*These hints for good housekeeping were included in the program
of the Royal Art Club in a Prairie View scrapbook kept by
Ethelyn Taylor Chisum around 1913.*

Prairie View and Houston's Texas Southern University were the only state-supported colleges for black Texans until the 1950s. Following the U.S. Supreme Court decision (*Sweatt v. Painter*, 1950) that segregated colleges and universities were unconstitutional, formerly white schools gradually began accepting black students.

Most parents sacrificed so their children could go to college. One woman recalled that "my grandmother ... worked very hard" to put six children through college. Another woman said, "My mother insisted that all of her children get a college education. She was a teacher herself," along with four of her sisters and brothers.

COLLEGE PRESIDENTS

Artemisia Bowden became head of St. Philip's College in San Antonio in 1902. In 1926, she was appointed president, the first woman in Texas to head a college. A few years later, in 1930, Dr. Mary Elizabeth Branch, the daughter of former slaves from Virginia, became president of Tillotson College in Austin until her death in 1944. When Dr. Branch first arrived on the campus, she had to fight her way through underbrush so thick that a fox was hiding there. The buildings were dilapidated and the library had only 2,000 books. She worked so hard and so diligently that within five years, she expanded the library to 21,000 books, renovated the buildings, and attracted hundreds of students. Under her leadership, Tillotson helped produce a new generation of well-educated black leaders.

In 1994, Dr. Carol Surles was installed as president of Texas Woman's University in Denton. She is the first African American woman to serve as head of the nation's largest university primarily for women. She said, "People don't really care what you know until they know that you care."

Dr. Mary Elizabeth Branch was the first woman in Texas to be president of a senior accredited college — Tillotson College in Austin.

CHAPTER 4

Community Building:
Women United!

If you are so focused on self,
you cannot have any awareness of the common good.

BARBARA JORDAN

B LACK women were most powerful when they came together for the good of their communities. They worked hard at community-building through their sororities, clubs, and churches. They made a big difference in the lives of children and those unable to care for themselves, and their charitable work reached all over the world.

CLUBS

MANY women's clubs first concentrated on cultural and literary programs, since black people could not use the all-white public libraries and had none of their own. Later the clubs expanded their efforts to help people of their own race who were in need. Austin women, many of them teachers, were founders of the Douglass Club in 1906. The club was named for the black newspaper editor, Frederick Douglass, a strong opponent of slavery and a supporter of women's rights. The Douglass Club is one of the oldest continuing women's clubs in Texas.

Travel was a problem in the days of segregation, so the women set up a network of hospitality in individual homes. When they traveled, they spent the night and shared meals with each other. Club women organized to help the poor, improve education, create an enjoyable social and cultural life, and take political action.

The Douglass Club of Austin was organized in 1906. The club women talked about books and helped others. Many of the founders were teachers.

SORORITIES AND YWCAS

FREDERICA CHASE DODD of Dallas helped start the Delta Sigma Theta sorority when she attended Howard University in Washington, D.C. The sorority was a "sisterhood" of young women who organized to make new friends and train to be leaders. In 1913, she and the other Deltas marched in a parade supporting suffrage on the eve of Woodrow Wilson's inauguration as President. When

Dodd returned to Dallas, she continued her sorority work and taught school. Her teaching career and work with church and club women became a stepping-stone for a new career in social work. During the Depression years of the 1930s, when times were hard and people had trouble finding jobs, Frederica Dodd ran a welfare office for blacks.

Members of Austin's Douglass Club collected money for the Salvation Army around 1940. Left to right: Mary Elizabeth Lewis, Mary Yerwood Thompson, and Mrs. Sadie Jones.

In the 1920s, Dodd worked with other black and white leaders to found a Young Women's Christian Association branch for African Americans, the Maria Morgan branch of the YWCA. This branch promoted better race relations, sponsored a summer camp, and held classes in cooking, nursing, and English. It helped black women find jobs and keep them. During the days of segregation, the YWCA was often the only place besides the church where blacks could hold meetings or social events.

Dr. Mamie L. McKnight,
a Dallas educator, has been
chancellor of the Dallas County
Community College District and
a founder of the historical society
Black Dallas Remembered.

INSTITUTIONS

IN 1937, the National Negro Health League of Galveston sponsored a special week to improve the health of families. Young people and their parents learned about the importance of regular exercise and dental care and also learned to cook nutritious meals.

During the Depression, many women with children wanted to work but said, "If I just had somewhere to leave my babies, I believe that I could get out and find a job."

The Community Welfare Association, an organization started by seven clubs for black women in Austin, decided to help out by providing a playground and then a nursery school for preschool children of unemployed parents. It furnished the school with tables, chairs, dishes, toys, and cots for naptime. The CWA also sponsored a city nurse and distributed milk to needy families.

Anna Dupree was a successful Houston businesswoman who founded a child-care center and a home for the aged. Dupree worked as a beautician in the 1920s and 1930s, making house calls to clients in white neighborhoods until she was prevented from doing so by a white beautician's group. She did not let this setback stop her. In 1936, she opened her own salon where she fixed hair and nails and also sold makeup, shampoos, and skin conditioners. As her business prospered, she and her husband, Clarence, did not forget those in need, and gave thousands of dollars to charities.

CHURCHES

CHILDREN helped build the Wesley Chapel African Methodist Episcopal (AME) Church in Georgetown, Texas. In 1904, Mrs. J. A.

Jones, the pastor's wife, organized them into the Nail Club. They raised enough money to buy all the nails for the new building. The church now has a Texas historical marker.

The majority of members of the early churches were women. Women often held services in their homes before congregations could afford buildings. They gave money and land to build places of worship, directed choirs, taught Sunday school, and played the piano and organ for services. They raised money for their churches by sponsoring barbecues and dinners on the grounds. They often were responsible for keeping the church building cleaned and repaired.

Texas women have been key figures in churches. They have taught Sunday School, played musical instruments, sung in the choirs, raised funds, and today are ministers.

Dr. Maud A. B. Fuller of Austin was a public schoolteacher for twenty-five years. She was also president of the Women's Auxiliary of the National Baptist Convention for forty years. Maud Fuller founded and edited a national newspaper, the *Woman's Helper*. She organized and wrote handbooks for black Baptist youth groups. She visited Africa several times, and in 1944 she raised enough money to build a mission in Liberia. She and her husband, William Handy Fuller, who ran a funeral home in Austin, adopted and helped educate twenty-five young men and women from many foreign countries.

Black teachers and ministers' wives were leaders in Christian education and missionary work. Women collected money, food, and living supplies to send to children attending African missionary schools. They also helped the homeless and poor in their own neighborhoods.

DR. GLORIA SCOTT:
THE FIRST BLACK PRESIDENT OF THE GIRL SCOUTS

Dr. Gloria Scott grew up in Houston. As early as the second grade, she had a paper route. Once she tried to sell a paper to a man who said he couldn't read. She told him, "Well, I could read it to you."

The one thing that really bothered her was that she couldn't use the whites-only public library. Finally, when she was a high school senior, the Houston public libraries were opened to blacks. She remembered, "I walked through every inch of the library."

Gloria Scott studied zoology in college. After graduation, she taught in college. In 1975, she was elected national president of the Girl Scouts of the U.S.A. in 1975, the first black woman to hold that position. She was presiding officer of the National Women's

Dr. Gloria Scott (upper right), the first African American president of the Girl Scouts of the U.S.A., at a National Council Meeting in 1978.

Conference in Houston in 1977. She said, "People ask me how I can be concerned with women's issues . . . it means a heavier burden on the energies of minority women because you are at one and the same time part of two minorities," blacks and women. She became president of Bennett College in Greensboro, North Carolina, in 1987.

CHAPTER 5

Fighting Oppression:
For the Vote and Against Violence

Fairness is an across-the-board requirement

for all our interactions with each other. . . .

Fairness treats everybody the same.

BARBARA JORDAN

EVEN though blacks won their freedom after the Civil War, they were still a long way from being treated as first-class citizens. They could not sit in restaurants outside the black community, ride in whites-only railroad cars, or even try on clothes in department stores. They could not use whites-only public libraries, attend whites-only public schools, or use the bathroom at most gas stations.

THE MEANING OF "JIM CROW"

"JIM CROW" laws and customs like these took away many of the rights gained after the Civil War. Jim Crow was the name of a white man who was the star of a minstrel show. He did a song and dance routine with his face covered in blackface makeup to resemble a black person. During his show, the audience shouted, "Jump, Jim Crow!" When segregation became widespread, the name "Jim Crow" became a popular way to describe the laws and practices of segregation.

VOTES FOR WOMEN

TEXAS women have acted when they have seen problems or felt they were treated unfairly. They worked to defeat Jim Crow and other unjust laws and practices.

After the Union troops came to Texas in 1865 and freedom was proclaimed for the slaves, black men got the right to vote. Black women could not vote, however, because they were women. As a matter of fact, no women were allowed to vote in any state of the Union. It would be fifty years until most U.S. women won that right.

Black men wanted their mothers, wives, sisters, and daughters to be able to vote. During the Texas Constitutional Convention of 1869, six out of the ten black delegates supported a resolution to grant the vote to women. Unfortunately, the Texas Constitution later adopted provided that all men could vote except idiots, imbeciles, the insane, and felons. Women were not even mentioned!

Black women like Christia Adair and Kitty Simmons joined with white women in Kingsville to work for women's suffrage—women's right to vote. They collected signatures on petitions urging legislators to pass suffrage laws. Unfortunately, in most other places, white suffragists would not work with black women or let them join their organizations.

Christia Adair worked with both black and white women in Kingsville to collect signatures on petitions demanding the vote.

In 1918, Texas granted women the right to vote in political party primary elections. Christia Adair, Kitty Simmons, and their friends in Kingsville eagerly went to the polls on primary election day to vote for the very first time. But an election official turned them away.

"Are you saying that we can't vote because we are Negroes?" Mrs. Simmons asked.

"Yes," he replied.

Christia Adair recalled that story almost seventy years later. "That just hurt our hearts real bad," she said. She and her friends did not let this setback stop them from fighting for equality and fairness. They knew that they deserved their rights as citizens. Finally, in June 1919, the Texas legislature became the first in the South to ratify the Nineteenth Amendment to the U.S. Constitution. It became known as the Susan B. Anthony Amendment, named after the woman who had worked so many years for its adoption. The amendment took effect on August 26, 1920. Women could now vote and run for office. They were citizens at last.

In 1920, three Houstonians became the first black women in Texas to run for public office. One ran for the legislature, one for the county school superintendent's position, and one for county clerk. They didn't win, but they made a respectable showing and they were pioneers.

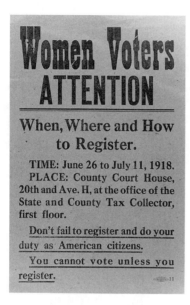

Women Voters
ATTENTION

When, Where and How
to Register.

TIME: June 26 to July 11, 1918.
PLACE: County Court House,
20th and Ave. H, at the office of the
State and County Tax Collector,
first floor.

Don't fail to register and do your
duty as American citizens.

You cannot vote unless you
register.

*In 1918, Texas women won the right
to vote in party primaries,
but the Democrats wouldn't
let black women vote because
of their color. In 1944, the
U.S. Supreme Court declared the
all-white primary unconstitutional.*

THE WHITE PRIMARY AND THE POLL TAX

AFTER the women's suffrage amendment passed in 1920, the Texas legislature came up with another discriminatory law. It passed the White Primary Act to prevent blacks from voting in Democratic Party primaries. But since the Democratic Party was by far the largest party in Texas, whoever won the primary always won the election. Not being able to vote in party primaries was almost like not being able to vote at all. In 1944, twenty-four years later, the U.S. Supreme Court finally ordered the Texas Democratic Party to allow blacks to vote in its primaries.

Everybody who wanted to vote still had to pay a poll tax, usually $1.75. Many poor people, black, white, and Hispanic, could not afford this amount. In 1966, the U.S. Supreme Court declared the poll tax to be unconstitutional. Today, no one has to pay for the right to vote.

The Republican Party showed prejudice, too. In 1920, Christia Adair and most other black Texans were Republicans, because that had been the party of Lincoln, who freed the slaves. When Presidential candidate Warren G. Harding came to Kingsville, Mrs. Adair took a group of black schoolchildren down to the train station to meet him. Her husband worked for the railroad, and he made sure that the car stopped right in front of his wife and her group. Imagine their disappointment when Harding, the important leader, reached over the black children's heads and shook hands with the white children. Christia Adair was so angry that she quit the Republicans and joined the Democrats.

VIOLENCE AND LYNCHINGS

BEING ignored by a presidential candidate was an insult. But many black Texans from the 1870s to the 1920s faced much worse. During the years after the Civil War, black families, like other families, wanted to live in peace. They worked hard, went to church, and tried to pay their bills. But some whites were so angry about the South losing the war that they began using violence.

The Ku Klux Klan tried to scare blacks from voting, owning property, going to school, or collecting wages. The KKK beat black men and women, covered them with tar and feathers, and killed them in vicious attacks called lynchings. Sometimes blacks were beaten for being too sick to work or working too slowly or "sassing" bosses. Even children were beaten. When Hannah Mullins's family rode the train through Bowie, Texas, in the late 1800s, they had to "lean way back in their chair with the blinds pulled down," or Klansmen might shoot at them through the window.

WOMEN PROTEST

SOME women complained to the Freedmen's Bureau, which was an agency set up by the federal government to protect freedpeople. Around 1868, a Dallas woman named Rachel complained to a bureau agent after she was knocked down and whipped by her employer, who didn't like the way her newly baked bread tasted.

Other women took legal action to protect their rights. Millie Anderson filed suit in federal court against the Houston and Texas

Central Railroad because they denied her a seat in a railroad car reserved "for white ladies only." She won the case in 1875.

Many women used their strength and courage to defend themselves and their families, even though it was very dangerous to do so. One woman in Village Creek, near Waco, was so angry at the attacks by the Klan that she threw burning embers from her fireplace on them the next time they rode by.

In 1919, a Dallas family was forced to leave town. Zelma Watson George, the teenage daughter of a Baptist minister, was at home taking care of her five brothers and sisters while her parents were at the courthouse trying to free an innocent black youth. A delegation of Klansmen, who wore white bedsheets to cover their heads and bodies, banged on the front door. They threatened, "You and your family better be out of town in forty-eight hours." The family left for Kansas. She recalled, "In those days, we knew what happened if we ignored the Klan." Dr. Zelma George later represented the United States in the United Nations, winning an award for her outstanding service.

In 1922, the Klan pressured sixty black families in Denton to move away from a college for white girls (now Texas Woman's University). The people and their houses were to be physically removed from the site. One black woman, Mrs. Mary Ellen Taylor, refused to leave voluntarily. As the movers pulled her house away to a new location, she remained seated inside, rocking away in her favorite chair.

Although individual acts of resistance against violence and the Klan were important, women began organizing as well. Mrs. Ethel Ransom was a Fort Worth nurse and club leader who became the Texas director of the national Anti-Lynching Crusaders. This organization was formed in 1922 to recruit "One Million Women United to Suppress Lynching" and to raise one million dollars for education and lobbying. That was quite a large sum of money in those days. Other black women's organizations—sororities, church and club groups, and the YWCA—also joined together to fight lynching. A white Texas woman, Jessie Daniel Ames, organized the Association of Southern [White] Women against Lynching in 1930. They, too, opposed these outrages.

Mrs. B. J. Covington was a Houston leader of the Texas

Mrs. B. J. Covington was a leader of the Texas Commission on Inter-racial Cooperation, which opposed lynching. She also founded the Blue Triangle YWCA in Houston to provide a meeting place for women and girls.

Women were leaders of the Dallas Progressive Voters League.
Mrs. Minnie Flanagan chaired a successful membership and
voter registration campaign in the late 1930s.

Commission on Inter-racial Cooperation. In the 1920s, many black
and white women and men worked together to achieve sisterhood
and brotherhood in this new organization. The TCIC accom-
plished small but important victories, such as founding kinder-
gartens and Boy Scout troops and providing free lunches for young
children. They helped young women find jobs and persuaded the
legislature to open a state orphanage and a home for delinquent
black girls, many of whom were homeless.

Mrs. I. W. Rowan and other black home demonstration agents were told to use the freight elevator when they tried to attend a convention in Dallas at the Adolphus Hotel in 1933. They refused.

In the 1930s, violence died down, but other outrages were still widespread. Mrs. I.W. Rowan was state superintendent for black home demonstration agents in Texas. These agents were key professionals who helped families improve their crops, manage their money wisely, and prepare and preserve nutritious food.

In 1933, black home demonstration agents from all across the state were invited to join their white colleagues at a conference at the Adolphus Hotel in downtown Dallas. When they arrived, they were ushered to the basement and told to take the freight elevator instead of the main elevator in the lobby. They refused to submit to such humiliating treatment and left the hotel. When the convention leaders invited them to return, they went home instead.

CHAPTER 6

Work:
Women of Achievement

A true story. A woman preparing for a large party had
pressed her yard man into household service.
As they attacked the many tasks, she expressed second thoughts
about the social event because of all the effort entailed.
His response was weak in grammar, but the message was powerful:
"Ain't nothin' worth nothin', that ain't no trouble."

BARBARA JORDAN

I N 1910, almost fifty years after freedom was won, most black women still worked on farms and as domestic servants and laundresses. Because of discrimination in education, they could not easily move into professions. Since Congress passed civil rights bills in the 1960s, more black women have been able to complete college and advance in business, the professions, and government service.

Dr. Yvonne Ewell was the first black female associate superintendent of schools in Texas (1976). She was elected to the Dallas school board in 1987, and served as vice president.

DAREDEVIL OF THE SKIES

WHEN is work the most fun? When you are lucky enough to be working at something you love. Bessie Coleman loved flying, but it was not just luck that set her blazing across the skies. Though she was one of the first licensed female pilots in the world and the first black aviator, she was born in a house with a dirt floor in Atlanta, Texas, in 1892. The family soon moved to Waxahachie. Bessie's mother borrowed books from a traveling library so that her daughter could teach herself to read.

Bessie moved to Chicago to live with her brother in 1915. Then the air war in Europe attracted her attention, and she decided to become an aviator. When she tried to find a flight school, she discovered that none of them accepted women. She later recalled, "I would not take 'no' for an answer." She had to go to France to study.

In 1921, Bessie Coleman became the first black woman in the world to receive a pilot's license from the International Aeronautics Federation. She went back to Chicago and performed in air shows to raise money for her own flying school. Her dream was to teach aspiring young women to fly. The shows were popular with blacks and whites throughout the South, in a time when blacks could not ride alongside whites in buses, trains, or streetcars.

In 1926, when Bessie Coleman was thirty-four years old and on the verge of opening her own flying school, she died in a plane crash while performing in Florida. A careless mechanic had left a wrench loose, and it jammed her controls. She is not forgotten, though—black aviators named clubs and magazines after her, and one of the main drives leading to Chicago's O'Hare Airport is named Bessie Coleman Drive. In 1995, the U.S. Postal Service issued a commemorative stamp in her honor as part of its Black Heritage Series.

*Bessie Coleman, a native of
Atlanta, Texas, was the first black
woman in the world to earn
a pilot's license.*

PUBLIC HEALTH PIONEERS

DR. Charles Yerwood, an Austin doctor, wanted his two daughters,
Connie and Joyce, to become musicians. But from the days when
they were little girls riding beside him in a horse and buggy as he
made house calls, the two sisters knew they would be doctors too.
At that time, all Texas medical schools were closed to black students, but this did not stop them. They saw one black woman in the
photograph of their father's graduating class at Meharry Medical
College in Nashville, Tennessee. Inspired by her example, Connie
and Joyce Yerwood attended Meharry to get their professional edu-
cations. They were awarded doctor of medicine degrees in 1933.

In 1937, Dr. Connie Yerwood Connor was appointed as the first black physician on the staff of the Texas Department of Health. She specialized in preventive medicine and worked hard as she traveled thousands of miles to rural communities, opening clinics for pregnant women and infants and children. She also helped train midwives at a time when most Texas babies of all races were born at home. Over the years, Dr. Yerwood was repeatedly passed over for promotions. After the Civil Rights Act of 1964, she was finally promoted to be the first black director of Maternal and Child Services in Texas, and later the first black chief of the Bureau of Personal Health Services.

Dr. Connie Yerwood Connor was the first black physician on the staff of the Texas Department of Health. She became director of Maternal and Child Health Services after the Civil Rights Act was passed in 1964.

Her sister, Dr. Joyce Yerwood Carwin, practiced medicine for fifty years in New York and Connecticut, treating low-income women and children. A clinic was named for her in Stamford, Connecticut.

Dr. Judith L. Craven was the first black woman to graduate from Baylor University College of Medicine in 1974, launching a highly successful career in public health. She was chief of anesthesiology for Riverside General Hospital in Houston. She became the second black director of the Houston Health Department and was dean of the School of Allied Health Sciences at the University of Texas Health Science Center in Houston. In 1992, she became the second woman and the first African American to serve as president of the United Way of the Texas Gulf Coast.

Dr. Judith Craven directed the Houston Health Department and was a university dean. She worked to help prevent teens from becoming pregnant.

NURSES AND MIDWIVES

NURSES as well as midwives practice their healing arts to care for the sick and save lives. Midwives deliver babies, stay with mothers and new babies, and assist doctors in delivery. Nellie Brown was a popular midwife in the Victoria area. Once when she was faced with a difficult birth, she brewed tea from a baby wasp's nest for a woman who reportedly drank it and "birthed her baby without no trouble a-tall." Home remedies such as these sometimes worked very well. Another midwife, Matilda Boozie Randon, delivered almost all the babies, black and white, in Washington County. She carried a black bag, just like the doctors, and was well respected.

HOME DEMONSTRATION AGENTS

HOME demonstration agents, appointed from about 1915 on, were professionals who taught women to plant gardens, cook nutritious food, make mattresses, beautify their homes, landscape their property, and protect themselves from disease. Mrs. E. G. Jones, a home demonstration agent from McLennan County, visited women's homes and taught them to make and sell hooked rugs. One woman made ten rugs and earned nine dollars in profits. In the 1930s, Waller County women learned to can. They preserved "815 cans of corn, 218 cans of okra, 150 jars of tomato preserves, 9 gallons of chow chow, 114 jars of canned peaches, 75 jars of peach preserves, and 50 jars of jelly made from peach peels."

Have you ever caught a cold from sharing a drink with another schoolmate? Dr. Jeffie O. A. Conner, a home demonstration supervisor and educator in Waco, noticed that children drinking water from the same dipper were catching colds and other diseases from each other. She taught them to make sanitary drinking cups from used tin cans instead of drinking from the same dipper. The children improved their health by making 1,700 drinking cups from tin cans they otherwise would have thrown away. They were expert recyclers.

Dr. Jeffie O. A. Conner was a home demonstration supervisor and educator in Waco.

BUSINESSWOMEN

OTHER women opened small businesses, such as cafés and ice cream parlors, laundries and grocery stores, rooming houses and boarding houses. Some were milliners and seamstresses. They used their domestic skills in many of these businesses.

The new profession of beautician attracted many women in the early 1900s. Over the years, women of all ethnic groups have opened their own beauty shops. Augustine Williams was the first black female director of examinations for the Texas Cosmetology Commission, from 1972 to 1984. She then went into business for herself, establishing the Style Rite Beauty Shop in Austin.

Lucille Bishop Smith was a Prairie View A&M University home economics professor. She set up the first commercial foods department at the college level and developed the first hot roll mix in the United States. Her hot roll mix and other products she created were so successful she decided to incorporate a business. She founded a family corporation in 1974 at the age of eighty-two. One of her best customers was the heavyweight champion Joe Louis.

Alice Taylor King established the King Funeral Home in Austin in 1933 with her husband, Charles B. King, and earned her own funeral license by passing a state examination. She operated this family business into her seventies and even played the organ for all the chapel funerals.

BREAKING NEW GROUND

AFTER Congress passed civil rights laws in the 1960s, more black women began entering professions formerly dominated by men. Today, more and more young women of all ethnic groups are studying mathematics, science, and computer technology.

Iola Johnson was one of the first television anchorwomen in Texas. She anchored programs on WFAA-TV, Channel 8, the ABC affiliate in Dallas, from 1973 to 1985.

Francine Frazier Floyd used electronic equipment in her job with Motorola in Austin. She was named Black Engineer of the Year in 1991.

Louise Martin became interested in photography at age eleven when her mother bought her a camera. She was soon taking pictures of her fellow students for her school yearbook in Brenham. She wanted to be a photographer, but because she was black, no white southern schools were open to her. She saved her money from domestic work to pay her tuition at the University of Denver, where she earned a degree in photography. She also studied at the Art Institute and American School of Photography in Chicago. In 1952, Louise Martin exhibited her work for the Southwestern Photographers convention. Her photos had to be hung in the hotel mezzanine because blacks were not permitted to ride the elevators. She was not discouraged. "You have to have confidence in yourself," she said at the end of her forty-year career. Her photographs of the funeral of Martin Luther King, Jr., earned her national recognition.

Dr. Ruth Simmons became the first black woman to head a top-ranked college or university when she became president of Smith College in Northampton, Massachusetts, in 1995. She was born in Grapeland, Texas, one of twelve children in a sharecropping family which moved to Houston when she was seven. She grew up in a segregated society with a drive to excel which came from within. She said, "Although I didn't have shoes or toys or clothes . . . my mind, and what I poured into it, equalized all that. I knew that my

Francine Frazier Floyd was Black Engineer of the Year in 1991
and went to work for Motorola.

[69]

mind could take me anywhere." While she was a student at Dillard University in New Orleans, Simmons' brothers and sisters helped her financially. "Sometimes it would be $5, or $10. My teachers sent me money, too." After graduation from Dillard, Simmons received a master's degree and a doctorate in the Romance languages from Harvard University. She later worked as provost of Princeton University and provost of Spelman College in Atlanta, Georgia.

*Dr. Ruth Simmons (right) became president of
Smith College in Massachusetts in 1995.
Ada C. Anderson (left) is an Austin educator and civic leader.*

Ada C. Anderson is an Austin business, educational, and civic leader. She was a trustee of the Austin Community College, is a certified real estate broker, and founded LEAP (Leadership Educational Arts Program) to benefit black youth.

FIRST BLACK WOMAN IN SPACE

DR. Mae C. Jemison was the first African American woman astronaut, joining NASA (the National Aeronautics and Space Administration) in Houston in 1987. She had been selected from more than 1,800 applicants. At that time, five black men served as astronauts. A native of Alabama, Mae Jemison grew up in Chicago, where she was an honor student in high school.

Dr. Jemison has a background in both chemical engineering and medical research, as well as African and African American studies. In 1992, she was a science specialist on an eight-day NASA space mission cosponsored by the United States and Japan. On that mission, she was a coinvestigator on a bone cell research experiment. In describing her role as a "scientist-astronaut," she said, "Our responsibilities are to be familiar with the shuttle and how it operates, to do the experiments once you get into orbit, to help launch the payloads or satellites, and also do extra-vehicular activities, which are space walks."

After leaving NASA in 1993, Dr. Jemison established her own company in Houston. She previously served in the U.S. Peace Corps as a medical officer in West Africa. She is a student of the Russian, Swahili, and Japanese languages, and enjoys weight training, dance, and exercise, along with photography, sewing, and skiing.

Dr. Mae C. Jemison was the first black woman astronaut. She was a science specialist on an eight-day mission in 1992.

CHAPTER 7

World War II:
Serving Their Country

We seek to unite people not to divide them,
and we reject both white racism and black racism.

BARBARA JORDAN

B LACK women served their country in World War II by joining the military and working in defense industries. They also
conserved food and planted victory gardens.

IN THE MILITARY

ELIZABETH "TEX" WILLIAMS of Houston had a career as a
Women's Army Corps (WAC) photographer for twenty-six years—
from 1944 to 1970. She also worked as a laboratory technician and
a medical photographer. She often flew as the only woman on
Army Air Force maneuvers to photograph combat techniques.
"Tex" was the first female graduate of the Photo Division School at
Fort Monmouth, New Jersey. After the war, she was a photogra-
pher for defense intelligence agencies.

The war gave many black women their first chance to serve in
the military. Unfortunately, the Women's Army Corps at that time
was officially segregated. When the first group of thirty-nine black
volunteers arrived at Fort Des Moines, Iowa, in 1943, to be sworn in
as WACS, they were called "colored girls" and told to move to the
other side of the room from the white women. They were segregated from whites and housed in their own barracks. Many black
soldiers, both men and women, were outraged at their treatment.
Black soldiers were fighting and dying to combat fascism overseas

[74]

Elizabeth "Tex" Williams
of Houston was a photographer in
the Women's Army Corps from
1944 to 1970.

while their brothers and sisters faced second-class treatment at home. The clamor for democracy and civil rights picked up steam.

Mary Bingham August Anderson joined the armed forces at the age of forty-one, the oldest in her group. When she went to Houston's City Hall to volunteer, the recruiters called her "Pee Wee" and told her to go home because she was only four feet, eleven inches tall. She refused to go. "You asked for cooks," she replied, "and I am an experienced cook." Her job in the military was to teach black and white cooks the tricks of the trade. Many of them "didn't know you had to let the water boil for three minutes" to make coffee, she said.

Annie Lois Brown Wright, Ruth L. Freeman, Geraldine Bright,
and Alice Marie Jones (left to right) were graduates of
Prairie View A&M. They wanted to serve their country during
World War II, so they volunteered. At the WAC facility in Iowa
they earned the equivalent rank of second lieutenant.

Black women also served in the Army Nurse Corps. Finally, in 1948, President Harry S. Truman issued an executive order commanding the full integration of black nurses into the armed forces. Second Lieutenant Leola Green of Houston spent almost a year of active duty nursing in North Africa. When she returned home in December 1943, she told a reporter for the *Houston Informer*, "An injured soldier ceases to be black and white in the fighting force." When a life was in danger, this brave nurse did not pay attention to the color of a soldier's skin.

ON THE HOME FRONT

ON the home front, children participated in the war effort also. At Prairie View College, 4-H club girls knit clothing for the soldiers fighting overseas. Young people helped their mothers make garments for the Red Cross and collected tinfoil and scrap metal for the war effort.

Young people boosted morale during World War II by entertaining military forces and the folks back home. Sorority members

Young people helped boost the morale of visiting soldiers and those back home by performing musical programs.

and club women worked in USO (United Service Organization) centers and sent candies, food, and letters to the soldiers and sailors. They also bought thousands of dollars' worth of war bonds.

Members of 4-H clubs worked hard to support the war effort. They grew their own fruits and vegetables so that extra food could be sent to the military forces. These plots of land were called victory gardens. Some food items like meat and sugar were rationed during the war.

4-H club girls in Washington County, Texas, raised baby chicks to improve the diets of black families through the Victory Farm Program. Texas poultry production rose from fifth to second in the nation in 1942. Children also learned to conserve food so that surplus goods could be sent abroad.

During World War II, female students at Prairie View Normal Institute took courses in radio communication, radio engineering, internal combustion engines, drafting, and industrial mechanics.

During World War II, female students at Prairie View took courses in engineering and industrial education.

AT WORK

GLADYS HUMPHERY worked at a meat processing plant in Fort Worth. During the war, women processed cuts from hogs, cattle, and sheep. They also stretched and dried hides. These jobs had been done by men before they were called away to help fight the war. Humphery canned chili, vienna sausage, and hot tamales, put lids on cans, and sliced bacon. She was such a good worker that she was soon promoted to be an inspector. In her new job, she was responsible for grading, separating, and packing bacon, as well as labeling cartons for shipping. She was also a leader in her union—the United Packing House Workers of America—which helped workers get better wages and health benefits.

Women also took the place of men in other important jobs. An all-woman locomotive washing crew worked in Kingsville during the war. The women cleaned boxcars, swept, handled freight, and washed and steamed the engines.

Olivia Rawlston and other black women worked in a garment factory in Dallas making military uniforms. They used power machines and were also pressers, collar-setters, and sleeve-makers. Although many of the workers in Olivia Rawlston's factory were blacks, all the forewomen were whites. Rawlston was president of the segregated section of her union—the International Ladies' Garment Workers Union (ILGWU)—one of the oldest unions with predominantly female members in the country. She was the first black delegate from the South to attend an ILGWU convention, held in Boston during the war.

Because of their wartime experience in jobs which had previously been closed to them, many women learned that they could be good industrial workers. After the war was over, most of the women were forced out to make room for returning military men. They were the last to be hired and the first to be fired. But they would make use of the skills and experience they had acquired in the war jobs in other ways later in their lives.

Olivia Rawlston and other Dallas women helped the war effort by sewing military uniforms. Rawlston was president of the segregated branch of the International Ladies' Garment Workers Union.

CHAPTER 8

The Civil Rights Movement:
Equal Justice for All

The majority of the American people still believe that
every single individual in this country is entitled to
as much respect, just as much dignity, as every other individual.

BARBARA JORDAN

Dᴜʀɪɴɢ the days of segregation, "White People Only" signs were posted at public water fountains, swimming pools, public libraries, and even at city halls all across Texas, in towns large and small. Black people could not use the same facilities as white people. One Houston park had a sign that read:

THIS PARK WAS GIVEN

FOR WHITE PEOPLE ONLY.

MEXICANS AND NEGROES STAY OUT.

ORDER OF PARK BOARD.

Signs like this infuriated citizens of color, who paid taxes but were unable to use certain public facilities.

FIGHTING SEGREGATION

Bʟᴀᴄᴋ men and women—and many white and Hispanic supporters—began challenging these laws and practices because they believed they violated the U.S. Constitution. They organized through groups like the ɴᴀᴀᴄᴘ (the National Association for the Advancement of Colored People). After years of struggle and the growth of the civil rights movement, in the 1960s the U.S. Congress finally passed a series of laws to correct these problems. As a result of this legislation, some black women were able to move as far as their talents would take them and were no longer tied to jobs as domestic workers. If a woman wanted a higher-paying job in business or industry or government, she could compete with other applicants to advance her career, and it was illegal to discriminate against her. Blacks were also beginning to be elected to public office in greater numbers.

Dr. Dorothy Redus Robinson experienced the effects of segregation but lived long enough to see victories won. She taught for almost fifty years in the Texas public schools. When she caught a train in 1944 during World War II from San Francisco to Bay City, Texas, Dorothy Robinson had a humiliating experience. "White prisoners-of-war, German, I suppose, were marched under guard through my coach to enjoy a meal in the dining car to which I had been denied admittance," she recalled.

Because the University of Texas refused to admit her, Dorothy Robinson drove her car more than 10,000 miles back and forth between her home in Palestine, Texas, and San Francisco State Teachers College, where she earned a master's degree. In 1950, the U.S. Supreme Court ruled that colleges and universities must be desegregated. She was finally able to enter the University of Texas for a summer course in 1955.

Dorothy Robinson's struggles demonstrate, in one woman's life, what the civil rights movement was all about. A highly intelligent woman, she could not attend the college of her choice close to her home. When she traveled by train, she could not eat in the dining car. And when she drove, she could not stop and use restroom facilities in service stations. She and other black citizens could not sit down in the waiting rooms of airport, train, or bus stations, but were segregated into spaces with few and sometimes no facilities. They could not enjoy a hamburger or a cold drink at a whites-only lunch counter or use the same drinking fountains as whites in department stores. Something had to be done, and many brave black women joined others in changing the laws. Dorothy Robinson and her husband Frank Robinson were active in the NAACP. And Dorothy Robinson continued to teach—she taught almost fifty years.

NAACP LEADERS

CHRISTIA ADAIR fought for more than seventy years to win suffrage and civil rights for black Americans. When Christia and her husband Elbert Adair moved to Houston in the 1920s, she began working for civil rights. She joined the NAACP in 1925 as recording secretary of the Houston branch. She said, "I never can remember the day when I wasn't liberated. Negro women have always been in a position to work and do things that they wanted to do."

After her husband's death in 1943, Christia had to go to work. She was hired by Lulu B. White, another NAACP leader, as a paid assistant in the Houston office. When the organization ran out of money in 1949, Christia continued working for little or no pay.

One of her pet peeves was the Houston airport. She remembered, "Negroes could not sit in the waiting room, get a cold drink, couldn't go buy a cold soda water or anything at the counters or concessions." When the city requested federal funds for a new airport, Christia and the NAACP complained about discrimination. After all, black people paid taxes to the federal government just like everyone else. Why couldn't they use tax-funded facilities? Finally,

OPPOSITE: *Dorothy Redus Robinson taught for almost fifty years in the Texas public schools—most of the time during segregation. She is shown here with her last class of students in Palestine, Texas, in 1974, on her sixty-fifth birthday.*

just before the new airport opened in 1953, Christia persuaded the
new mayor that blacks should have equal access to the facilities.
She and the NAACP won that battle. They also succeeded in getting
the Houston public libraries opened to blacks.

Juanita Craft of Dallas, the granddaughter of slaves, devoted
forty years to winning equal rights for African Americans. She
joined the NAACP around 1935, shortly after a state tubercular hospital for whites only refused to admit her dying mother. Craft was
an organizing genius who helped found dozens of NAACP
branches in Texas.

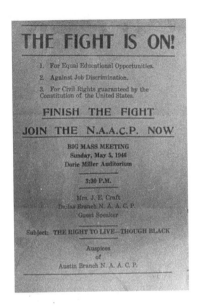

THE FIGHT IS ON!

1. For Equal Educational Opportunities.
2. Against Job Discrimination.
3. For Civil Rights guaranteed by the Constitution of the United States.

FINISH THE FIGHT

JOIN THE N.A.A.C.P. NOW

BIG MASS MEETING
Sunday, May 5, 1948
Dorie Miller Auditorium

3:30 P.M.

Mrs. J. E. Craft
Dallas Branch N. A. A. C. P.
Guest Speaker

Subject: THE RIGHT TO LIVE—THOUGH BLACK

Auspices
of
Austin Branch N. A. A. C. P.

Juanita Craft used this flyer to advertise her speeches as she traveled around the state organizing for the NAACP.

She also organized youth groups to clean up Dallas neighborhoods and recycle tin cans and bottles. They helped integrate the State Fair of Texas. Juanita Craft recalled, "They were discriminating against my kids. They used to have just one day (Negro Day) a year when we could go. I went out there one day with the kids, and the little white kids were buying tickets to go on the Midway. The little Negro kids were just looking. That stirred me up. We had placards and everything. The best one was, 'Don't trade your pride

OPPOSITE: *Juanita Craft of Dallas helped organize dozens of NAACP chapters throughout Texas.*

for a segregated ride.' We tried to buy Coca-Cola. They wouldn't sell us that. We tried to buy sandwiches. They wouldn't sell us that. I still get angry when I think of what we had to go through to straighten things out."

She registered voters and conducted "Get Out the Vote" drives. One year, she sold over 1,000 poll taxes. (At that time you had to pay $1.75 to vote in Texas.) She used the slogan "The fight is on" to publicize her speeches as she traveled around the state organizing NAACP branches. At the age of seventy-three, Juanita Craft ran for the Dallas City Council and won, serving two terms. In 1984, she received the Eleanor Roosevelt Pioneer Award from Texas Woman's University.

✓ **Juanita Craft** will fight *AGAINST* the proposed increases in our gas and electric bills

✓ **Juanita Craft** will fight *AGAINST* the proposed new telephone charges for calling information

✓ **Juanita Craft** will fight *FOR* our fair share of city services and funds to protect and improve our neighborhoods

Elect Democrat Juanita Craft
CITY COUNCIL — DECEMBER 23RD
Pol. Adv. Pd. By Mrs. M. H. Jackson, Campaign Treas.

This is one of the advertisements Juanita Craft used to win election to the Dallas City Council in 1975. She served until 1979.

GETTING ELECTED

IN 1958, Mrs. Charles E. White (Hattie Mae White) of Houston became the first black Texan elected to public office in the twentieth century. She was the wife of an optometrist and a champion for integrating the public schools. Hattie Mae White had been a teacher, a PTA leader, and a mother of five, so she felt that she was well qualified to run for the Houston school board. Her platform included better school buildings, federal aid for school lunch programs, and peaceful integration. She won the election with the help of voters from different ethnic groups working together.

Hattie Mae White was the first black person elected to public office in Texas during the twentieth century. In 1958, she was elected to the Houston school board.

A week after her election, some person filled with hate shot rifle bullets through her car windshield. A cross was also burned in her front yard. These frightening events did not stop Hattie Mae White. She continued her courageous struggle to help schoolchildren. In 1965, the school board finally adopted the federal free milk program, which she had supported for many years. She served until 1967.

INTEGRATING COLLEGES AND UNIVERSITIES

HATTIE BRISCOE was the first black woman to graduate from St. Mary's School of Law in San Antonio. For twenty-seven years, she was the only black woman attorney in the area. Her mother, who encouraged her to get as much education as she could, said, "I want all my kids to rub their heads against the college walls." Hattie Briscoe was an honor student in high school. She worked her way through Wiley College in Marshall by washing, ironing, and cooking. She taught school and was a beautician and cosmetology instructor for many years.

When she decided to enroll in law school, she worked as a clerk-typist at Kelly Air Force Base in San Antonio during the day to support her night studies. During her first semester, she was told that women had no business being there. "I am a woman, I am in law

school and I am going to become a lawyer," she answered. She made the Dean's List every semester, and her dream came true when she graduated number one in her law school class. The year was 1956, and she was forty years old.

Hattie Briscoe of San Antonio was the first black woman to graduate from a Texas law school (1956).

During the civil rights movement of the 1960s, many students not only went to class and did their homework but also worked for integration. Even though it was almost 100 years since slavery had ended, most white-owned businesses refused to serve black customers on the same basis as whites. Black and white students "sat in" together at segregated lunch counters throughout the South, insisting that the black students be served.

One civil rights victory gave blacks their first chance for an education equal to whites. Prairie View had opened in 1879; for sixty-eight years it was the only school available for Texas blacks wanting public higher education. Black taxpayers helped to support the University of Texas and other state schools, but they could not attend them.

In 1882, Texas voters, black and white, voted by a two-to-one majority to open a state university for blacks in Austin. The legislature did not vote to provide the funds for such a school until 1947. The newly funded school, Texas State University for Negroes, was located on the site of a former junior college for blacks in Houston. TSUN later became Texas Southern University. Its most prominent graduate was Barbara Jordan, who served in the U.S. Congress.

The University of Texas opened its doors in Austin to white students in 1883, but did not admit black undergraduates until 1956. It was the first major state university in the South to do so.

When Vivienne Malone-Mayes applied for entrance to Baylor University in Waco in 1949, she was refused admission because she was black. She attended Fisk University in Nashville, Tennessee, instead. After the U.S. Supreme Court ruled that colleges should be integrated, she entered the University of Texas at Austin and was one of the first blacks there to earn a doctorate in mathematics. Her earlier slight from Baylor did not stop her. In 1966, Dr. Malone-Mayes returned to Baylor as the first black professor at the school which had once refused to admit her.

IN PUBLIC PLACES

MABLE M. CHANDLER was one of the founders of Interested Women in Dallas. This group of strong black women worked to open local department stores and restaurants to blacks. They were angry because when they went shopping, they were not allowed to try on clothes they were interested in buying. Their children couldn't try on shoes, shirts, or blue jeans either. Mable Chandler and members of her sorority, the Alpha Kappa Alphas, recruited three hundred other black women to close their charge accounts and burn their credit cards. They refused to buy any new clothes for Easter in 1961. Finally, when the stores saw that their sales were slipping, they gave in. The owners then decided to let black citizens try on clothes. The women celebrated with a shopping trip in August.

Mable M. Chandler organized the Interested Women in Dallas to open department stores and restaurants to black citizens.

In 1962, Ada C. Anderson organized the Mothers Action Council to integrate the Ice Palace, an Austin skating rink. Bertha Means and many other Austinites joined in. When the Ice Palace opened in September in the center of the black community, the managers had told blacks that they and their children would not be welcome. The children were very disappointed, as they had been looking forward to the fun of ice skating for months. MAC mothers and their children, along with white allies, marched and picketed in front of the Ice Palace for a whole year—every day, every night, and on weekends. Anderson recalled that they continued their protest "through rain, sleet and snow until the owners dropped the racial barriers."

Brave women indeed!

In 1962, Ada C. Anderson (right) organized the Mothers Action Council in Austin to integrate an ice skating rink. Many Austin citizens like Bertha S. Means (left) helped her.

CHAPTER 9

The Arts and Sports: Creating and Performing

Art has the potential to unify. It can speak in many languages without a translator. Art does not discriminate—it ignores external irrelevancies and opts for quality, talent and competence.

BARBARA JORDAN

Why does sport matter so much? Sport is an equal-opportunity teacher. It is a nonpartisan event. It is universal in its application. It is almost a cliché to say there is no "I" in the word "team."

BARBARA JORDAN

THE ARTS

TALENTED black women have built careers in the arts—painting, music, writing, theater—despite many obstacles. Black women have emphasized their African American heritage in their art, accenting the spiritual in everyday practices. Their works spring from daily life and love of family, and sometimes in response to discrimination or segregation.

PAINTING

Naomi Polk was one woman whose expression could not and would not be held back. Polk, an important self-taught painter, was the youngest of ten children. She started school before the turn of the century, but had to drop out early to baby-sit the children of her older sisters while they worked. She always regretted her lack of schooling. She sold cosmetics and homemade insecticides during hard times to supplement her small welfare checks and support herself and her two children. She decorated their home by painting designs of flowers and butterflies on orange juice cans and then filling them with plants.

Naomi Polk considered writing and art to be her life's work. She was up by four or five o'clock in the morning to write, and then she stayed up late at night painting after the day's chores were done.

She mixed her own paints and worked on materials she found, like cardboard, ceiling tile, scraps of wood, and old window shades.

No one outside her family saw her paintings until after her death in 1984 at age ninety-two. Her art is now featured in museum exhibits and private collections. In one of her best-known poems, "My Little Ghetto Kitchen," Polk describes her "flowered cottage kitchen curtains with designs of pineapples, pears, and you-name-it things," and "the blessed sunshine" that "brings a message of love on its wings."

*Alma Gunter painted scenes of daily life in East Texas,
like* Dinner on the Ground, *a church picnic.*

Alma Gunter was a nationally known painter who first made her living as a nurse. She began painting seriously after her retirement in 1978, depicting scenes of daily life in East Texas. Her paintings include many delightful childhood memories: washdays, kitchen activities, and waiting for the iceman in summer. (In Gunter's childhood, ice was delivered for iceboxes before the days of electric refrigerators.) She said, "I paint what my mind photographed and recorded over all the years of my life."

ART COLLECTING

When Aaronetta Pierce was a docent at the San Antonio Museum of Art in 1980, a young black girl gazed up at her and said, "Mrs. Pierce, there's something wrong here. Why don't I see pictures of black people?" Pierce and her husband, Dr. Joseph A. Pierce, Jr., decided to do something about that. They founded Premier Artworks, Inc., to market the works of African American artists, including paintings, drawings, sculpture, and limited edition prints. The pieces sell for as little as $300 and as much as $300,000.

The writer Maya Angelou called Aaronetta Pierce "a national treasure." Pierce was the first chair of the Martin Luther King Memorial City/County Commission in San Antonio, chaired a committee which led to the creation of the San Antonio Department of Arts and Cultural Affairs, and was a panelist for the National Endowment for the Arts. She is a member of the Texas Women's Hall of Fame.

Aaronetta Pierce of San Antonio
is a national leader of the arts.

MUSIC

Black women have always performed music to enrich their lives. They have carried their songs from the fields to their employers' houses, to their own houses, and from the country to the city. The music they have created reflects the places where they work, play, and worship—the kitchen, the nursery, the church, the schoolroom, the dance hall, and the concert hall.

Black musicians have enjoyed a variety of musical expression—spirituals, jazz, gospel, rhythm and blues, and classical. Much black music came out of the church, and before that, from the farms and fields. Singer Osceola Mays performed songs her mother and grandmother, a former slave, sang in the fields: "All they had to make music with was their mouths." Mays, born around 1911, sang songs she had learned as a girl for sixty or seventy years. She is featured in *Living Texas Blues*, a tape and accompanying book funded by the Dallas Museum of Art.

Mrs. B. J. Covington organized the Ladies Symphony Orchestra in Houston around 1915 to encourage her daughter Jessie Covington to be a musician. The orchestra was composed of black women and girls.

Jessie, who was a violinist in the Ladies Symphony Orchestra, decided to pursue a profession as a pianist. She graduated from the Oberlin Music Conservatory in Oberlin, Ohio, and the Juilliard School of Music in New York City. She developed a concert career, touring the South. She later married the president of Dillard University, Dr. Albert W. Dent, in New Orleans. There she encouraged music and the arts.

Etta Moten Barnett moved beyond church music to pursue a career on Broadway. The daughter of a minister, she began singing in her father's church choir in Weimar, Texas. She had roles in Hollywood feature films and played the female lead in George Gershwin's *Porgy and Bess* in the 1940s. She played Bess for three years, longer than any other professional actress. She said, "If you were a minister's daughter like I was, then you were in the theater. Being born in a church is almost like being born in theater."

Barbara Lynn of Beaumont and Port Arthur is a musician in the blues and gospel traditions. The *Austin American-Statesman* called her a "soulful singer-songwriter, mean left-handed guitarist." Lynn began touring at age fourteen. During the early days of her career, she wrote most of her own songs while performing in Texas and Oklahoma. Atlantic Records produced her blues-tinged rock hit "If You Should Lose Me" in 1963 while she was still in her teens. In the 1990s, she began appearing again in concerts sponsored by Texas Folklife Resources.

Metropolitan Opera star Barbara Conrad of Pittsburg, Texas, faced discrimination as an opera student at the University of Texas at Austin in the 1950s. She was not allowed to play a romantic role opposite a young white man.

Barbara Conrad of Pittsburg, Texas, was a vocal music student at the University of Texas in the 1950s. Her voice was so fine that she won a leading role in the university's opera production, costarring with a blond male student. Some members of the Texas legislature objected to the two races being cast opposite each other in romantic roles and threatened the university's funding. Barbara Conrad was forced to withdraw from the opera. She persisted in her musical career and became a Metropolitan Opera star in New York. Her performances have also been praised in European cities such as London, Vienna, and Hamburg.

The Leadership Educational Arts Program, or LEAP, was founded by Austin civic and cultural leader Ada C. Anderson

Anne Lundy of Houston founded the Scott Joplin Chamber Orchestra, the first in the country to specialize in performing the works of black composers.

under the auspices of the Austin Lyric Opera in 1989. The program makes it possible for young people to experience the community's many cultural opportunities and travel to events nationwide. LEAP encourages young performers as well as those interested in cultural enrichment.

Christine Fanuel (left) and Muriel Archer (right) enjoyed walk-on roles in the Austin Lyric Opera's production of La Bohème *in 1992. The teenagers were participants in* LEAP, *Leadership Educational Arts Program, an enrichment program founded by Ada C. Anderson.*

A TALENTED FAMILY

Poet Vivian Ayers Allen received a Pulitzer Prize nomination at the age of twenty-seven. She published an anthology of poems, *Spice of Dawn*, in 1953, and her poetry appeared in Langston Hughes's collection *New Negro Poets, USA* in 1964. She raised her children in

Houston before moving to Mount Vernon, New York, where she founded and is director of the Adept New American Museum. Vivian Allen is the mother of multitalented artists Phylicia Rashad and Debbie Allen, whose talents she nurtured from their youngest days. Vivian Allen's son, Andrew "Tex" Allen, is a jazz composer and musician.

Poet and museum founder Vivian Ayers Allen received a Pulitzer Prize nomination for her poetry at the age of twenty-seven.

Phylicia Rashad has said of her mother, "Everything we do and are we attribute to her. She's a scholar, a writer, an artist." Rashad is most famous for her role as Claire Huxtable, costarring with Bill Cosby on the popular television series *The Cosby Show*. Her mother advised her, "Be true, be beautiful, be free." Rashad told *Jet* magazine in 1990, "The Claire Huxtable you see on television is modeled after my mother." As a singer and dancer she has headlined from Las Vegas and Atlantic City and has appeared in the soap opera *One Life to Live.* Rashad is an award-winning actress who has performed on the Grammy Awards, in addition to roles in the Broadway plays, *Dream Girls* and *The Wiz,* among others.

Phylicia Rashad is best known for her role as Claire Huxtable, costarring with Bill Cosby on The Cosby Show.

Debbie Allen of Houston said, "Momma was raising us in the midst of segregation and racism to be independent and free." She "just made the Museum of Fine Arts our playground. We grew up

Emmy Award winner Debbie Allen of Houston is a versatile actress, singer, dancer, choreographer, and director for stage, television, and film.

loving music and art and dance. . . . Our mother always reared us to be free human beings and free spirits and understand that we were part of a universal community. . . . We never felt any boundaries about what we do, how far we could reach."

Allen is an actor, director, singer, dancer, and choreographer, sister of Phylicia Rashad and daughter of Vivian Ayers Allen. Their father, dentist Andrew Allen, encouraged their projects, including dance lessons. Before launching a career in show business, Debbie Allen majored in classics at Howard University. She debuted on Broadway in the chorus of *Purlie*, going on to other productions, including *Raisin*, *Ain't Misbehavin'*, and *West Side Story*. She directed, choreographed, and produced the television series *Fame*, for which she won two Emmys and a Golden Globe Award.

Naomi Carrier (left), a Houston teacher and poet, composed the songs and lyrics for I Am Annie Mae, *a musical based on the life of Annie Mae Hunt of Dallas (right). Mrs. Hunt went from farming and domestic work to becoming a self-employed seamstress and cosmetic saleswoman.*

LITERATURE

Ada DeBlanc Simond has helped preserve the history of the Austin black community through oral histories, a column in the *Austin American-Statesman*, and working with her sorority, Delta Sigma Theta, to produce an exhibit. She wrote books for children, the *Let's Pretend* series, based in part on the true stories of her friend, Marguerite Lewis, called Mae Dee.

Ada Simond, a native of Louisiana, learned to read early from her mother, who used the catechism in the Catholic prayerbook as a textbook. She was unable to attend school very often because she had to help care for her five younger brothers and sisters. "I was responsible for doing much of the work," she said. But she loved books and was soon reading difficult authors like Shakespeare. She recalled that after her family moved to Austin, black children in the segregated schools used old books discarded by white schools and books which their teachers brought from home. "The library was downtown and didn't admit us." Finally, in the 1940s, through the efforts of Ada Simond and other citizens, a library was opened in East Austin, where most African Americans lived at that time.

Ada Simond continued to study, at Samuel Huston College and then at out-of-state colleges to obtain a master's degree in home economics and child development. She worked for the Texas Tuberculosis Association as a health program specialist for twenty-five years and, upon retirement, took a job as a bailiff for the district court in Travis County.

ARCHITECTURE

Dr. Nia Dorian Becnel was an architect specializing in African influences on buildings constructed by slaves and other early black workers. She headed historic preservation studies at the University of Houston. When Dr. Becnel was doing graduate study in architecture at the University of Houston, she was told that women could not conceptualize, or create a mental picture, of space. She said, "If anybody can conceptualize space, we can. We've dusted it, repaired it and cleaned it."

SPORTS

BLACK women athletes have excelled in many sports both at the high school and college levels and professionally. Title ix of the 1972 federal educational amendments to the Civil Rights Act of 1964 provided many opportunities for young women of all ethnic groups in college athletic programs. It helped them on the way to Olympic and professional sports careers.

Black female Olympic medalists from Texas include Benita Fitzgerald-Brown, gold for 100-meter hurdles, 1984; Sandra Farmer-Patrick, silver in track and field, 1992; and Clarissa Davis, who shared the bronze in 1992 with the All-American basketball team. Gymnast Stephanie Woods, an Austin high school student, won three gold medals at the Pan American Games in Havana, Cuba, in 1991.

At age seventeen Zina Garrison of Houston became the first black player to win the junior singles tennis championship at Wimbledon, England. She has won many other awards as well.

Sheryl Swoopes of Lubbock was named National Collegiate Athletic Association Player of the Year in 1993. In 1996, she became a member of the U.S.A. Basketball's Women's National Team. The first female athlete to have a Nike sneaker named after her (Air Swoopes), Sheryl formerly played for the Lady Raiders of Texas Tech University in Lubbock. She holds four Southwest Conference

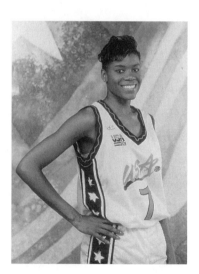

Sheryl Swoopes of Lubbock was a member of the 1996 U.S.A. women's Olympic basketball team.

single-season records, scoring a record-breaking forty-seven points in the final game of a National College Athletic Association championship game.

Swoopes's hoop dream started in Brownfield, a small West Texas town, where she learned to play basketball wearing her two older brothers' hand-me-down sneakers. She played on the travel court her brothers built in their yard. They couldn't afford a rim or backboard, she remembered, "So we stuck an old board into the ground. For the rim, we used a bicycle wheel and took the spokes out. That was our goal." She said that she wasn't even supposed to graduate from high school. "We didn't have money, we didn't have anything. And even if I graduated from high school, I was supposed to have one or two kids before I graduated. But that didn't happen." Instead, Sheryl went to college, earned a degree, and won a national championship. She overcame many obstacles on her road to stardom.

Carlette Guidry, a sprinter at the University of Texas at Austin, was named Southwest Conference Athlete of the Year in 1990 and was a member of the 1996 U.S.A. Women's Track and Field Team. She cruised to the best time in the world that year in the Olympic trials semifinals. Her time was 22.29 seconds in the 200-meter dash.

Barbara Jean Jacket is a legend in track and field. She was the first and only full-time female athletics director in the seventy-five-year history of the Southwestern Athletic Conference. She served as head women's track and field coach at Prairie View A&M

Carlette Guidry, a sprinter at the University of Texas at Austin, was named Southwest Conference Athlete of the Year in 1990.

for thirty-one years. Under her leadership, the Lady Panthers captured over twenty national titles. Fifty-seven of her student-athletes were named All-Americans. For five years she was the school's athletics director. In 1992, she coached the u.s. track and field team at the Barcelona Olympics. In 1995, Jacket was inducted into the International Women's Sports Hall of Fame in New York.

CHAPTER 10

Law and Politics: Women of Power

Those who hold the public trust must adhere
to the highest ethical standards there are.
The job requires it, and the public must demand it.

BARBARA JORDAN

A FRICAN American women in Texas have held some of the state's highest offices—they have been judges, legislators, school board and city council members, and congresswomen.

INFLUENCE OF THE CIVIL RIGHTS ACT OF 1964

THE Civil Rights Act became a gate through which black women could march toward opportunity in all fields. Taking advantage of each new chance for advancement, women entered many professions in greater numbers. They made the political process work for them by running for public office and serving in important appointed political posts. These achievements are especially important because so many people were against women of color having political power. Battles are still being fought for full representation, but the women are not afraid.

The first black Texas woman to be a major success in state and national politics was Houston attorney Barbara Jordan, who was elected to the Texas Senate in 1966. In 1972, she was elected to the U.S. Congress. She carved a path for many women to follow. Through 1994, nine more African American women were elected to the Texas legislature and two more to the U.S. Congress. They were all members of the Democratic Party.

If you look at a one-dollar bill printed from 1977 to 1980, you'll see the signature of Azie Taylor Morton, President Jimmy Carter's appointee as the first black Treasurer of the United States. Her signature appears on all U.S. currency printed during her years in office.

Azie Taylor Morton was the U.S. Treasurer from 1977 to 1980.
Her signature appeared on all money printed during those years.

CONGRESSWOMEN

EDDIE BERNICE JOHNSON

Nurse, Businesswoman, Health Care Administrator,
and Lawmaker

In 1972, the year Barbara Jordan was elected to Congress, Eddie Bernice Johnson was elected by a landslide to the Texas House of Representatives from Dallas County. She was the first black woman ever elected to public office in Dallas. During her three terms as a House member, she sponsored a maternity leave bill for teachers, a breakfast bill for schoolchildren, and child care legislation, along with support for the state's Equal Legal Rights Amendment. In her second term, she became the first woman to chair a major committee—the Labor and Employment Relations Committee. She resigned during her third term when President Jimmy Carter appointed her as Regional Director of the Department of Health, Education and Welfare, supervising a five-state area from 1977 to 1979.

Eddie Bernice Johnson of Dallas was elected to the U.S. Congress in 1992. She is a registered nurse who also served in the Texas House of Representatives (1973–1977) and Texas Senate (1987–1993).

In 1986, there was another "first" for Eddie Bernice Johnson. She became the first black to represent Dallas in the Texas Senate. She worked on child care, drug-related crime, health, housing, literacy, and disability issues. In 1992, she was elected to the U.S. Congress with 74 percent of the vote, and reelected to a second term in 1994. She was elected Whip of the Congressional Black Caucus. Her priorities have included affordable health care, the environment, education, and jobs.

Before entering government service, Johnson had attended Notre Dame University in Indiana, then Texas Christian University in Fort Worth, where she earned a nursing degree in 1955. She was hired sight unseen for a psychiatric nursing job at the Veterans' Administration hospital in Dallas. "When I showed up black, they were just *shocked*," she recalled, and the discrimination was heavy-handed. Yet within a year and a half she was promoted to head nurse. As a civic leader, Johnson was the founding president of the National Council of Negro Women in Dallas and active in the Texas Women's Political Caucus. Eddie Bernice Johnson has worked hard to succeed in the face of many obstacles. She feels that "Women, indeed, have made a difference in Texas politics." She advises young women, "as well as young men, to get a very good education."

SHEILA JACKSON LEE

Attorney, City Councilwoman, Judge, and Congresswoman
Sheila Jackson Lee, a Houston attorney, was elected to the U.S. House of Representatives from Harris County in 1994. Soon after

her election, the *Houston Defender* said that she was "making waves on Capitol Hill." Lee was elected president of the Democratic Freshman Class and appointed to the House Democratic Steering and Politics Committee. She serves on the Committee on the Judiciary and a subcommittee on Space and Aeronautics and Basic Research. Key issues of concern to her are welfare, jobs for youth, housing for the homeless, and programs to help the elderly. She stands up for what she believes in. She said, "I don't believe that my constituents sent me to Washington to be intimidated. The key is that you're there to assure that the voices of your constituents are heard."

Sheila Jackson Lee, a Houston attorney, was elected to the U.S. House of Representatives in 1994 from Harris County.

Before coming to Congress, Sheila Jackson Lee was the first black woman at-large member of the Houston City Council and served as an associate municipal court judge. A graduate of the University of Virginia School of Law, she is only one of three black women to have served as director of the State Bar of Texas.

TRAILBLAZERS

WILHELMINA DELCO
Speaker Pro Tem

Wilhelmina Delco served Travis County in the Texas House of Representatives for twenty years—from 1975 to 1995. She was appointed Speaker Pro Tem, the number two position in that body, in 1991. She was the first woman and the second African American ever to hold that office. Visitors to the Capitol who saw her presiding at the podium often asked, "Who is that woman and what is she doing?" Delco said, "I realized how important it was for women and children particularly to walk in that House and see a woman in charge." As she completed her legislative career, she noted that times are changing. "I think there are more and more . . . girls in high school and college, wanting to be governor, wanting to be president," she said.

[119]

Wilhelmina Delco was a member of the Austin school board before being elected to the Texas House of Representatives. She served there from 1975–1995, and was appointed Speaker Pro Tempore, the number two position.

Delco's public service career began when she was elected student body president of her high school in Chicago. When she and her husband, Dr. Exalton Delco, moved to Austin, she served as PTA president while their children were small. In 1968, she became the first black woman elected to the Austin school board. "The real catalyst for her involvement was her children, starting with Girl Scouts and PTA," remembered her daughter Loretta Edelen, on the Austin school board herself in the 1990s. Delco helped found Austin Community College in 1973 and served on its first board of trustees.

In 1974, Delco decided that most educational problems could be solved only at the state level, so she ran for the legislature and won. Among those who helped her raise funds was future governor Ann Richards. Wilhelmina Delco chaired the House Higher Education Committee for twelve years. She spearheaded the passage of a state constitutional amendment which provided more funds for Texas's historically black public universities, Prairie View and Texas Southern.

In 1990, Delco chaired the South Africa Task Force of the National Conference of State Legislatures. She convinced the delegates to vote unanimously to continue economic sanctions in order to defeat apartheid (the separation of blacks and whites in South Africa).

To young people interested in a political career, Wilhelmina Delco has given some advice—advice that she herself has followed: "Find some person or some cause which you believe in and walk in and offer to help."

GABRIELLE MCDONALD
A Federal and International Judge

Gabrielle McDonald was the third black woman in the United States and the first in Texas to be a U.S. District Court Judge. She had previously worked as an attorney for the NAACP's Legal Defense and Education Fund in New York before moving to Texas in 1969. At that time, she challenged discriminatory practices at major companies across the state. She was the only black and female lawyer to appear in the federal courts there on a regular basis.

Gabrielle McDonald in 1979 became the first black woman in Texas to be a federal judge. She presided over a famous case concerning fishing rights in the Gulf of Mexico involving Ku Klux Klan–backed whites and Vietnamese-Americans.

Her most famous case as a district judge in Harris County in 1979–1988 was a dispute between Vietnamese-Americans and Ku Klux Klan–backed whites over fishing rights in the Gulf of Mexico. She and her family received threatening letters and phone calls during this period. But she was not intimidated. She ordered the Klan to shut down its paramilitary camps.

In 1991, Gabrielle McDonald joined the law faculty at St. Mary's

University in San Antonio. In 1993, she became a presiding trial judge for the International Criminal Tribunal for the former Yugoslavia, which is the United Nations' official Bosnian war crimes court. She is one of only two women on the eleven-judge tribunal, and the only one from the United States. She has an apartment in The Hague, in the Netherlands, but calls Houston home.

MYRA MCDANIEL

Secretary of State

Myra McDaniel became the first black Texas Secretary of State when she was appointed in 1984 by Governor Mark White. On January 15, 1985, she became the first black ever to call a Texas House of Representatives opening session to order.

Myra McDaniel was the first black Texas Secretary of State.

SENFRONIA THOMPSON AND KARYNE CONLEY

State Legislators

Senfronia Thompson of Harris County was elected to the Texas legislature in 1972, the same year as Eddie Bernice Johnson. An attorney, she has served longer in the Texas House than any other woman. She and other female legislators worked hard in 1973 to get a law passed allowing women to get credit in their own names without having to get the signatures of their husbands or fathers. In 1995, after sixteen years of struggle, she succeeded in obtaining the passage of an alimony law, which provides financial support for divorced women with little income.

Before her election, Thompson taught science and math in junior and senior high schools. She then decided to become a lawyer, attending classes between legislative sessions until she passed the bar examination and got her law license.

State Representative Karyne Jones Conley of San Antonio is a graduate of Harvard University. She was first elected to the Texas House of Representatives in 1988. She has been reelected three more times. Before her election, she worked for civil rights leader and U.S. Ambassador Andrew Young, served on the San Antonio School Board, and taught at San Antonio College.

Balancing office holding and family life, Conley, a wife and the mother of four children, decided to commute between San Antonio and Austin during legislative sessions. She has put 140,000 miles on her car in a few years. By commuting, she is able to have breakfast with her family, participate in legislative debates and committee hearings, and still return home in time for her children's school activities and dinner.

In discussing the values of leadership, she said, "I can't be a player [in the Texas legislature] if it means that I have to compromise my position and my principles, and you have to decide . . . if you want to be a part of the leadership, you gotta give up a lot of yourself. All of my votes are cast on what I believe in."

DR. ZELMA GEORGE
U.N. Leader

In 1959, President Dwight D. Eisenhower appointed Dr. Zelma Watson George as a member of the u.s. delegation to the United Nations. In 1961, she had done such an outstanding job that she

Dr. Zelma George of Hearne and Dallas was a member of the u.s. delegation to the United Nations from 1959 to 1961. She won an award for outstanding contributions to international understanding.

won the Dag Hammarskjöld Award for Contributions to International Understanding. Dr. George had many careers during her long life of ninety years. She was a sociologist, an educator, a musicologist, an opera singer, a lecturer, and a human rights advocate. In her later years, being in a wheelchair did not stop her. In 1982, she joined a march against nuclear weapons and then flew to Europe for the opening of the Vienna Opera.

CHAPTER 11

Barbara Jordan:
Defender of the Constitution

My faith in the Constitution is whole, it is complete, it is total.

BARBARA JORDAN

O N February 21, 1936, Dr. Thelma Patten went to her cousin's house in Houston's Fifth Ward to deliver a baby. The new baby, Barbara Charline Jordan, was the third of three daughters. Her parents, the Reverend Benjamin Jordan and Arlyne Patten Jordan, were both known in their community as fine orators in the Baptist Church. Dr. Patten was, herself, the first black woman doctor in Houston and one of the first in Texas. So young Barbara Jordan grew up in a family of firsts and fine speakers. One day she would be both.

GRANDPA PATTEN

THE Good Hope Missionary Baptist Church was an important part of the Jordan family's life. Barbara also learned a lot from grandfather John Ed Patten, who liked to read to her from his favorite books. He would drive his mule-drawn wagon while he searched the streets of Houston to collect good usable junk that other people had thrown away. Barbara liked to ride with him, and while she helped him sort old rags and paper for resale, he talked to her as if she were a grownup.

Grandpa Patten told her it was all right to be different from her

Barbara Jordan, who was born in Houston, is standing between her sisters Bennie amd Rose Mary.

friends. He advised her to "trot your own horse and don't get in the same rut as everyone else." He said, "Just remember, the world is not a playground but a schoolroom. Life is not a holiday, but an education. One eternal lesson for us all: to teach us how better we should love." These were lessons Barbara took very seriously. Despite living in a segregated city, Barbara learned to love instead of to hate. And she also learned that she wanted to do what her grandpa wanted her to do—to try to "travel up from segregation," to make the world a fair place for everyone in it.

In Houston at that time, as in all the states in the South, black people were segregated from white people by law and custom. All the schools Barbara and her sisters Bennie and Rose Mary attended in Houston were segregated. Barbara recalled, "It wasn't only the school system, it was everywhere. The church, the city. We would ride on the back of the bus."

Barbara Jordan, a native of Houston,
is shown here at age ten.

A CHAMPION DEBATER

At Phillis Wheatley High School (named for the black poet who had lived in Boston during the American Revolution), Barbara's favorite activity was the debate team. Members had to prepare to argue either side of an argument. On the debate team, Barbara learned some of the skills of oration that she would continue to sharpen as she got older. She was also very good at sizing up her competition. As a result, she won many awards for oratory. She was the only girl on the team, and she loved to debate the side against segregation. "I did not think it right for blacks to be in one place and whites in another place and never shall the two meet," she remembered later.

COLLEGE CHOICES

After hearing a speech by Judge Edith Sampson of Chicago, Barbara decided to become a lawyer. In 1952, when she graduated from high school, black students had several choices about where to go to college in Texas. They could go to one of the two state-supported colleges for blacks, Prairie View A&M or Texas Southern University (TSU), or to a private black college. Barbara later explained that TSU's original name was Texas State University for Negroes: "It was created to keep blacks out of the University of Texas." Even though the U.S. Supreme Court had ruled in the 1950 *Sweatt v. Painter* decision that segregation in higher education was unconstitutional, white institutions resisted admitting blacks. Not until 1954 did the University of Texas admit black undergraduates.

TEXAS SOUTHERN UNIVERSITY

Barbara chose to attend TSU, right in her hometown. She was elected president of the Delta Sigma Theta sorority, enjoying the informal times when she and her sorority sisters sang and put on skits.

She also joined the TSU debating team. But first she had to convince the coach that it was all right for her to travel around the country with him and the male team members. To fit in better, she wore high necklines, boxy jackets, and flat shoes. The team packed fruit, sandwiches, and fried chicken while traveling through the South because they were not sure of being able to find black-owned cafés, and they knew they would not be allowed to eat in white-owned restaurants. Segregation meant that they would even have trouble finding bathrooms they would be allowed to use. Despite these many obstacles, Barbara led the debating team to many victories.

Barbara first competed against white women in an oratory contest at Baylor University in Waco, Texas. When she won easily, she realized that "some black people could make it in this white man's world, and that those who could had to do it." Her proudest moment was when her team tied with Harvard University, a school with much more money and more debating experience than TSU.

BOSTON UNIVERSITY LAW SCHOOL

After graduating from TSU *magna cum laude* in 1956, with a degree in political science, she decided that she would go to a mainly white law school in the North. She chose Boston University Law School, where she was a double minority: she was a black and she was a woman. Out of six hundred students, only six were women, and only two were black women. These two black women, Barbara Jordan and Issie Shelton, were the only women who graduated with their class. The other four did not.

In law school, Barbara had to study very hard because the world the other students had grown up in was so different from hers. She realized that she had been deprived of more than she once thought. Even the best training available in an all-black university like TSU was not equal to that which her new friends had experienced. She knew she would have to read more and work harder than most of the white students, who already knew many legal terms and had had more exposure to opera, symphonies, and art museums. She and the other black students formed their own study group to help each other. Barbara also learned how to make friends with white people. She remembered that "white people love to stop whatever they're doing and go have a cup of coffee."

The contrast between her life in law school and her life before was more evidence of what she had known in her heart since she had listened to her grandfather — that it was wrong for people to be treated as inferior because of the color of their skin. She also learned a lot about the Constitution of the United States, and that there were words in it, like "liberty and justice for all," that she intended to take very seriously.

A LAWYER AT LAST

AFTER she finished law school in 1959 and became licensed to practice law in Massachusetts and Texas, Barbara Jordan decided to come home, where people in Houston needed her. For two years, to save money, she practiced law from her parents' dining room table. She then shared a small office with two friends. In 1960, she worked on the campaign to elect John F. Kennedy as President of the United States and Lyndon B. Johnson, a fellow Texan, as Vice President. Her speeches on their behalf were so well received that by the time their campaign ended in victory, she had been bitten by the political bug, as she put it.

ENTERING POLITICS

Barbara Jordan's parents, Arlyne and Ben Jordan,
were very proud of her victory in the Democratic
primary election to Congress in May 1972.

No BLACK woman had ever been elected to the Texas legislature before, but that did not stop Barbara Jordan. A lot of people in the early 1960s thought it was not normal for a woman to want to be in politics instead of at home with a husband and family. But that did not stop Barbara Jordan. She said to herself, "The question you have to decide, Barbara Jordan, is whether you're going to fly in the face of what everybody expects out there . . . or whether you can bring the public along to understand that there are some women for whom other expectations are possible." She ran for the Texas House of Representatives twice—in 1962 and 1964. She lost both times. But that did not stop Barbara Jordan.

After her losses, she thought about moving to another state, where a black woman would have a better chance of winning. But her home was Texas, so she decided to remain in her native state and keep trying.

Then two things happened that really made a difference. First, the U.S. Congress passed the Civil Rights Act of 1964. This was important because it outlawed discrimination in employment and segregation in public places like restaurants and bus stations. Second, Congress passed the Voting Rights Act of 1965. There were many places in the South where blacks were still not allowed to vote. In other places, election districts (the geographic areas that legislators represent) were not fairly designed, making it difficult, if not impossible, for blacks to win elections.

THE FIRST BLACK WOMAN
IN THE TEXAS SENATE

AFTER the passage of the Voting Rights Act in 1965, some of the election districts in Houston had to be drawn all over again. It was no longer legal to put all the black people in districts where white people's votes would outnumber them and determine who got elected. When a new district was drawn to send a senator to the

Texas legislature from Houston, Barbara decided to try again. The new district, a single-member district, had mostly black voters in it, and Barbara won an overwhelming victory two to one.

On May 27, 1967, Barbara Jordan was sworn in as the state's first black state senator since 1883. She recalled:

The senate is a small body in Texas. Thirty-one members. Those thirty men didn't know what to expect of me and I certainly didn't know what to expect of them. But everybody in my district . . . was very excited, especially the black people, because they had never thought that they would have a representative in the state capital of Austin. And so they closed the town down to come to Austin to see me take the oath of office and as I looked up into the Senate gallery, there was a sea of black people all scrubbed and cleaned up and happy. And when I walked down to the floor, they started to applaud. And that was a violation in rules of the Senate, and I know that, and I just put my finger to my lips, and the applause ceased. It was a very, very exciting day.

Jordan realized that she, the only woman and the only black person in the Texas Senate, might find it difficult to become an insider. But that was her goal. "As an insider," she said, "you would have some effect on the legislation, you would be able to do things for your constituency. . . . The best way to become a player in the Senate was to become friends with my colleagues and not make them uncomfortable because there was a woman in their presence."

She was so successful at making friends and demonstrating her abilities that she was named the outstanding freshman senator. In 1972, Jordan was unanimously elected president pro tempore (temporary president) of the Senate, a very visible position. When the governor and lieutenant governor left the state on June 10, Barbara Jordan served as acting governor for the day. She arranged for all the students from the high schools in the Fifth Ward of Houston, which she represented, to travel to Austin to watch her being sworn in. In this honorary position, she was the first black chief executive of any state. Her father was on the platform with her that day. He died the next day.

Barbara Jordan helped commission the u.s.s. Doris Miller,
a ship named after a black Texas World War II hero.

SENATE ACCOMPLISHMENTS

During the six years Jordan served in the Texas Senate, she was very successful not only in making friends, but in getting important legislation passed. More than half the bills she introduced became law—a very good record. The passage of those laws helped minorities and women as well as others, including workers, who got a minimum wage. Her efforts also increased worker's compensation for job injuries, created the Texas Fair Employment Practices Commission, and increased legal rights for women.

THE FIRST BLACK TEXAN IN CONGRESS

IN 1972, when a new district opened for a seat in the United States Congress representing the Fifth Ward, Jordan ran for that seat and won it. In 1973, she became the first black woman from a southern state and the first black Texan ever to take a seat in Congress. Her old political friend, former President Lyndon B. Johnson, helped her get appointed to one of the most influential committees in Congress, the House Judiciary Committee. This appointment would lead to Barbara Jordan's finest hour as a defender of the Constitution of the United States.

In 1972, just six years after winning a seat in the Texas Senate, Barbara Jordan was overwhelmingly elected to the United States Congress.

WATERGATE HEARINGS

The House Judiciary Committee had the authority, granted by the Constitution, to investigate whether President Richard M. Nixon had committed any misconduct during the Watergate affair, a series of political scandals. If the committee members discovered that President Nixon had behaved illegally, they could vote to impeach him, or formally accuse him of wrongdoing. The Senate would then conduct a trial to determine whether to remove the President from office.

After hearing evidence from the people who testified before the committee, Jordan realized she would have to vote to impeach the President of the United States because of what he had done.

Although she was shocked at the idea of impeaching a President, she was even more shocked at the charges of his "high crimes and misdemeanors" and the threat they posed to the U.S. Constitution.

On July 25, 1974, her voice—a voice she had cultivated throughout her career as a debater and a legislator—was heard by the nation. Barbara Jordan was telling not only the people, but also the

Barbara Jordan electrified the nation with her impassioned defense of the U.S. Constitution. She spoke as a member of the House Judiciary Committee during the impeachment deliberations on President Richard Nixon in 1974.

President, that her faith in the Constitution was so great that for any-
one—even the President—to weaken it was a terrible thing to do.

These were the words that made her famous:

*"We the people"—it is a very eloquent beginning. But when the
Constitution of the United States was completed on the seven-
teenth of September in 1787, I was not included in that "We the
people." I felt for many years that somehow George Washington
and Alexander Hamilton just left me out by mistake. But
through the process of amendment, interpretation, and court
decision, I have finally been included in "We the people . . ." My
faith in the Constitution is whole. It is complete. It is total. I am
not going to sit here and be an idle spectator to the diminution,
the subversion, the destruction of the Constitution.*

Perhaps Barbara Jordan's words made an impact on the country
because her ancestors had once been slaves, and here she was,
telling the world that even the powerful President of the United
States was not powerful enough to ruin the Constitution. The
Constitution came first, she said.

The committee agreed that there were three reasons to impeach
the President. Barbara Jordan voted in favor of each reason. To
avoid being impeached and tried, President Nixon resigned
August 9, 1974.

The speech Barbara Jordan made revealed how important it was for her to be sure that people who once had been left out could expect to be included in the American dream of liberty and justice for all. She always worked toward that goal.

CONGRESSIONAL RECORD

During Barbara Jordan's three terms in Congress, she cosponsored bills to help older Americans, children, the environment, teachers, and the homeless. One of her finest achievements was getting a bill passed that extended voting rights to Mexican Americans. This required that ballots be printed in Spanish if more than 5 percent of voting-age citizens spoke that language.

She also spoke out for an Equal Rights Amendment to the Constitution, so that it would assure equality of the sexes. In 1975, during International Women's Year, Jordan spoke at a conference at the Lyndon B. Johnson School of Public Affairs in Austin. She told the women: "It is going to take long, hard, slow, tedious work. And we begin with ourselves. We begin with our own self-concept. The women of this world—and the women of Texas, and the women of the United States of America—must exercise a leadership quality, a dedication, a concern, and a commitment." Twenty years later, she was still discussing women's issues. In 1995, she praised the recently concluded United Nations Fourth World Conference on Women, held in Beijing, China, saying, "Human rights and the rights of women are the same thing."

ADDRESS TO THE DEMOCRATIC
NATIONAL CONVENTION

In 1976, Jordan became the first black and first woman to deliver the keynote address at the Democratic National Convention, held that year in New York. The crowd in Madison Square Garden went wild, and there was a spontaneous outcry to urge her to run for vice president. She refused to allow her name to be placed in nomination.

After six years in the U.S. Congress, Barbara Jordan had decided not to run for office again. She realized she was so well known that her opinions would be heard on issues of major importance. "I didn't need to be an elected public official in order to . . . address those problems in any national or global way," she said.

PROFESSOR AT LBJ SCHOOL

In 1979, Barbara Jordan became a professor at the Lyndon B. Johnson School of Public Affairs at the University of Texas at Austin, teaching courses in ethics and political values. She advised her students to "get into the political arena because it is in that arena that every facet of one's life is touched." She said, "I have faith in young people because I know the strongest emotions which prevail are those of love and caring and belief and tolerance."

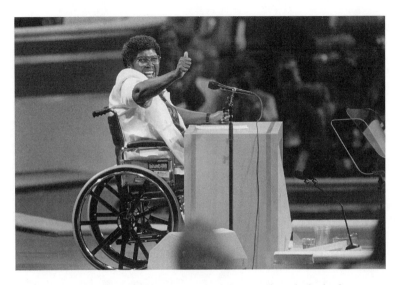

Barbara Jordan continued her busy schedule even though she had to use a wheelchair because of the disease of multiple sclerosis.

Her students called her BJ. Her classes were so popular that the school used a lottery to determine which students could enroll.

Unfortunately, she suffered from multiple sclerosis. As a result, she had to use a wheelchair. Despite that, Barbara Jordan continued her busy schedule of teaching, speaking, traveling, and public service. In 1991, Governor Ann Richards chose Jordan to be her special advisor on ethics. Said Jordan, "Ethical behavior means being honest, telling the truth, and doing what you said you were going to do. Listen to the still, small voice within you and you will probably do the right thing."

Barbara Jordan received a standing ovation following her keynote address to the 1992 Democratic National Convention in New York.

PRESIDENTIAL MEDAL OF FREEDOM

IN 1994, President Bill Clinton not only appointed Jordan chair of the U.S. Commission on Immigration Reform, but also awarded her the Presidential Medal of Freedom, the highest award possible for a civilian. Many other honors came her way: schools in Austin and Houston and a post office in Houston were named for her. She was elected to the Texas Women's Hall of Fame. She received twenty-five honorary degrees from colleges and universities all over the country.

HER LIFE

BARBARA JORDAN was a very private person, but she had a human side that the public did not always see. She loved to sing gospel and country songs at parties, play the guitar, and eat Mexican food, barbecue, and sweet potato pies. She also was an ardent fan of the University of Texas Lady Longhorns basketball team. She was present at many games cheering the team on.

In an interview shortly before her death, Barbara Jordan said:

I believe that diversity is in the legislative futures in each of the fifty states because we cannot stand to have, in a democracy, any significant portion of people who do not have a voice in what happens to them. All I know is that we as a people, Black, White, Asian, Hispanic, must keep scratching the surface until we get to where we got to be and that's all inclusiveness for all people.

Barbara Jordan died from pneumonia and complications of leukemia on January 17, 1996. She was buried in the Texas State Cemetery in Austin. She never lost sight of the values her family and her church taught her. She never forgot how important it was for everyone to have an equal chance to succeed. She never forgot the importance of the Constitution in making her achievements possible. Barbara Jordan always remained a defender of the Constitution.

*When Barbara Jordan died in 1996, the whole nation mourned
the passing of a great American.*

Barbara Jordan Chronology

1936	Born in Houston, February 21
1952	Graduates from Phillis Wheatley High School
1956	Graduates *magna cum laude* from Texas Southern University
1959	Graduates from Boston University Law School
1960	Teaches at Tuskegee Institute in Alabama
1961–1966	Practices law in Houston
1962, 1964	Runs (unsuccessfully) for Texas House of Representatives
1965	Appointed administrative assistant to Harris County Judge William Elliot
1966	Wins race for Texas Senate
1967	Sworn in, Texas Senate
1968	Wins four-year term to Texas Senate

1972	Serves as Governor for the Day, June 10
	Elected to U.S. House of Representatives
1973	Appointed to House Judiciary Committee
1974	Delivers famous speech about the Constitution
	Reelected to U.S. House of Representatives for second term
1975	Delivers keynote address to Democratic National Convention
1976	Reelected to U.S. House of Representatives for third term
1978	Retires from Congress
1979	Accepts Lyndon B. Johnson Public Service Professorship at Lyndon B. Johnson School of Public Affairs, University of Texas at Austin
1982	Accepts Lyndon B. Johnson Centennial Chair in National Policy at LBJ School of Public Affairs, UT
1985	Main Post Office in Houston dedicated to Barbara Jordan

1986   Named by *The World Almanac* as one of the
             25 most influential women in the United States

1991   Appointed Special Counsel for Ethics by
             Governor Ann Richards

1992   Delivers keynote address to Democratic National
             Convention

1994   Appointed by President Clinton as chair of
             U.S. Commission on Immigration Reform

1994   Awarded Presidential Medal of Freedom

1996   Dies in Austin, January 17

Sources of Quotations
by Barbara Jordan

PREFACE   Commencement Address, Harvard University, 1977.

CHAPTER 1   Keynote Address, National Democratic Convention, July 13, 1992.

CHAPTER 2   Remarks, Top Teens of America Conference, February 28, 1994, Austin, Texas, as quoted in *On Campus*, March 2, 1994.

CHAPTER 3   Malcolm Boyd, "Where Is Barbara Jordan Today?" *Parade Magazine*, February 16, 1986.

CHAPTER 4   Remarks, Symposium on Issues of Integrity in Athletics, University of Texas at Austin, April 7, 1994.

CHAPTER 5   Remarks at the exhibit "The Last Best Hope of Earth: Abraham Lincoln and the Promise of America," Huntington Library, San Marino, California, as quoted in *Los Angeles Times*, December 15, 1993.

CHAPTER 6   Remarks, Development and University Relations Seminar, University of Texas System, November 9, 1993.

CHAPTER 7   Keynote Address, Democratic National Convention, July 13, 1992.

CHAPTER 8 Remarks at a symposium, "The Johnson Years: LBJ: The Difference He Made," sponsored by the University of Texas at Austin and the Lyndon B. Johnson Library, May 3–5, 1990.

CHAPTER 9 Arts: From a 1993 lecture, quoted in *Austin American-Statesman*, November 2, 1994.
Sports: Remarks, Symposium on Issues of Integrity in Athletics, University of Texas at Austin, April 7, 1994.

CHAPTER 10 "Excellence in Leadership and Public Policy," Remarks, Inaugural Meeting of the Littlefield Society, University of Texas at Austin, February 22, 1991.

CHAPTER 11 U.S. House Judiciary Committee, July 25, 1974.

Reading List

Barbara Jordan Reader. Pamphlet for the exhibition "Barbara Jordan: Freedom Medalist and Texas Treasure." Capitol Visitors Center, Austin, January 12 – June 19, 1995.

Barr, Alwyn. *Black Texans: A History of Negroes in Texas, 1528–1971.* Austin: Jenkins Publishing Company, 1973.

Berry, Mary Frances, and John W. Blassingame. *Long Memory: The Black Experience in America.* New York: Oxford University Press, 1982.

Bryant, Ira B. *Barbara Charline Jordan: From the Ghetto to the Capitol.* Houston: D. Armstrong & Co., 1977.

Duren, Almetris Marsh, and Louise Iscoe. *Overcoming: A History of Black Integration at the University of Texas at Austin.* Austin: University of Texas, 1979.

Franklin, John Hope. *From Slavery to Freedom: A History of Negro Americans.* 5th edition. New York: Alfred A. Knopf, 1980.

Handbook of Texas, revised edition. Austin: Texas State Historical Association, 1996.

Hare, Maud Cuney. *Norris Wright Cuney: A Tribune of the Black People.* New York: Crisis Publishing Company, 1913; reprint, Austin: Steck-Vaughn, 1968.

Hine, Darlene Clark, editor. *Black Women in America: An Historical Encyclopedia.* 2 volumes. Brooklyn, N.Y.: Carlson Publishing Company, 1993.

Hunt, Annie Mae, and Ruthe Winegarten. *I Am Annie Mae: An Extraordinary Black Texas Woman in Her Own Words.* Austin: Rosegarden Press, 1983; reprint, Austin: University of Texas Press, 1996.

In Celebration of the Life of Barbara Jordan, 1936–1996. Memorial service program. University of Texas at Austin, January 28, 1996.

Jordan, Barbara, and Shelby Hearon. *Barbara Jordan: A Self-Portrait.* Garden City, N.Y.: Doubleday, 1979.

McKnight, Mamie L., editor. *First African-American Families of Dallas: Creative Survival.* Volume 1. Dallas: Black Dallas Remembered Steering Committee, 1987.

—————, and BDR Editorial Board, editors. *African-American Families and Settlements of Dallas: On the Inside Looking Out.* 2 volumes. Dallas: Black Dallas Remembered, 1990.

Museum of African-American Life and Culture. *They Showed the Way: An Exhibit of Black Texas Women, 1836–1986.* Dallas: MAALC, 1986.

Rawick, George P., editor. *The American Slave: A Composite Autobiography.* 41 volumes. Series 1, 7 volumes; series 2, 12 volumes; *Supplement,* series 1, 12 volumes; *Supplement,* series 2, 10 volumes. Westport, Conn.: Greenwood Press, 1972, 1977, 1979.

Rich, Doris L. *Queen Bess: Daredevil Aviator.* Washington, D.C.: Smithsonian Institution Press, 1993.

Robinson, Dorothy Redus. *The Bell Rings at Four: A Black Teacher's Chronicle of Change.* Austin: Madrona Press, 1978.

Seligman, Claudia Dee. "Ada Simond." In *Texas Women: Legends in Their Own Time,* pp. 37–45. Dallas: Hendrick-Long Publishing Company, 1989.

Simond, Ada DeBlanc. *Let's Pretend Series.* Austin: Stevenson Press [1970s].

Winegarten, Ruthe. *Black Texas Women: A Source Book.* Austin: University of Texas Press, 1996.

—————. *Black Texas Women: 150 Years of Trial and Triumph.* Austin: University of Texas Press, 1995.

—————. *Governor Ann Richards and Other Texas Women.* Austin: Eakin Press, 1993.

Credits

PHOTOS

PAGE 2   Archives Division, Texas State Library

PAGE 4   Photo by Dorothea Lange, Photographs and Prints
            Division, Schomburg Center for Research in Black
            Culture, The New York Public Library, Astor, Lenox
            and Tilden Foundations

PAGE 5   Austin History Center, Austin Public Library, pica 05994

PAGE 9   Courtesy Mrs. Annie R. Lee; print from University of
            Texas Institute of Texan Cultures, San Antonio

PAGE 10   George Washington Carver Museum

PAGE 15   Austin History Center, Austin Public Library, pica 05496

PAGE 17   University of Texas Institute of Texan Cultures,
            San Antonio

PAGE 19   Austin History Center, Austin Public Library, pica 05476

PAGE 21   Courtesy Steck-Vaughn Pub. Co. and Center for
            American History, University of Texas at Austin,
            CN 01748

PAGE 24   Victoria College Local History Collection

PAGE 27   Robert Morris, *Reading, 'Riting, and Reconstruction*
            [University of Chicago Press, 1981]

PAGE 30   Charles Tatum, *Shelby County* [Eakin Press, 1984]

PAGE 32   From the collection of the Texas/Dallas History and
            Archives Division, Dallas Public Library

PAGE 36   Huston-Tillotson College, Austin

PAGE 39   Courtesy Dr. Connie Yerwood Connor

PAGE 40   Courtesy Mary Yerwood Thompson

PAGE 41   Texas Black Women's History Archives, African
                   American Museum, Dallas

PAGE 43   Courtesy Rosenberg Library, Galveston

PAGE 45   Courtesy Girl Scouts of the U.S.A.

PAGE 50   Courtesy Willie Lee Gay; print from Ellen C. Temple

PAGE 56   Courtesy Houston Metropolitan Research Center,
                   Houston Public Library

PAGE 57   Texas Black Women's History Archives, African
                   American Museum, Dallas

PAGE 58   Permanent Collections—Archives/Special Collections
                   Department, John B. Coleman Library, Prairie View
                   A&M University

PAGE 60   Texas Black Women's History Archives, African
                   American Museum, Dallas

PAGE 62   National Air and Space Museum, Smithsonian
                   Institution [SI Neg. No. 84-14782]

PAGE 63   Courtesy Dr. Connie Yerwood Connor

PAGE 64   Governor's Commission for Women Archive,
                   The Woman's Collection, Texas Woman's University

PAGE 66   The Texas Collection, Baylor University, Waco

PAGE 69   Photograph by Tom Goodwin, courtesy
                   Francine Frazier Floyd

PAGE 70   Photo by Sharon Kahn

PAGE 72   National Aeronautics and Space Administration

PAGE 75   Courtesy Elizabeth "Tex" Williams

PAGE 76   Official W.A.A.C. photo, reproduced in the 1943 *Prairie
                   View Panther*, courtesy Permanent Collections—
                   Archives/Special Collections Department, John B.
                   Coleman Library, Prairie View A&M University

PAGE 77   Courtesy Rosenberg Library, Galveston

PAGE 78   Permanent Collections—Archives/Special Collections
           Department, John B. Coleman Library, Prairie View
           A&M University
PAGE 80   People's History in Texas
PAGE 84   Courtesy Dorothy Redus Robinson
PAGE 86   Craft [Juanita Jewel Shanks] Papers, Center for American
           History, University of Texas at Austin, CN 00674
PAGE 89   University of Texas Institute of Texan Cultures,
           San Antonio
PAGE 91   University of Texas Institute of Texan Cultures,
           San Antonio
PAGE 93   Texas Black Women's History Archives, African
           American Museum, Dallas
PAGE 94   Courtesy Ada C. Anderson
PAGE 97   Billy R. Allen Fath Art Collection, African American
           Museum, Dallas
PAGE 99   Photo by Cynthia Clark, courtesy Aaronetta Pierce
PAGE 101   Photo by Marc Raboy, courtesy Barbara Conrad
PAGE 102   Photo by Jeff St. Mary, courtesy Anne Lundy
PAGE 103   Courtesy Ada C. Anderson
PAGE 104   Courtesy Adept New American Museum,
           Mount Vernon, N.Y.
PAGE 105   Courtesy Adept New American Museum,
           Mount Vernon, N.Y.
PAGE 106   Courtesy Adept New American Museum,
           Mount Vernon, N.Y.
PAGE 107   Photo by Tomás Pantín, Austin
PAGE 110   Photo by Steven Freeman/NBA Photos
PAGE 112   © Susan Allen Sigmon, courtesy Women's Athletics Division,
           University of Texas at Austin
PAGE 115   The Woman's Collection, Texas Woman's University, Denton

PAGE 116   Courtesy Eddie Bernice Johnson
PAGE 118   Courtesy Sheila Jackson Lee
PAGE 120   Photo © Danna Byrom
PAGE 122   Courtesy Gabrielle McDonald
PAGE 123   Photo by Bill Malone
PAGE 125   Copy from University of Texas Institute of Texan
         Cultures, San Antonio
PAGE 129   Texas Southern University, Barbara Jordan Archives
PAGE 130   Texas Southern University, Barbara Jordan Archives
PAGE 135   Photo: *Houston Chronicle*
PAGE 138   Source: U.S. Dept. of the Navy; copy from University of
         Texas Institute of Texan Cultures, San Antonio
PAGE 140   Photo: *Houston Chronicle*
PAGE 141   Texas Southern University, Barbara Jordan Archives
PAGE 145   Photo: *Houston Chronicle*
PAGE 146   Photo: *Houston Chronicle*
PAGE 148   Photo by Larry Murphy, courtesy Office of Public
         Affairs, University of Texas at Austin

FIGURES

PAGE 52   Poster from Minnie Fisher Cunningham Collection,
         courtesy of Houston Metropolitan Research Center,
         Houston Public Library
PAGE 87   Texas/Dallas History and Archives Division, Dallas
         Public Library
PAGE 88   Texas/Dallas History and Archives Division, Dallas
         Public Library

Index

Adair, Christia, 49, 50, 51, 53,
    85–86
Adept New American Museum,
    104
Allen, Andrew, 106
Allen, Andrew "Tex," 104
Allen, Debbie, 104, 105–107
Allen, Vivian Ayers, 103–104, 106
Ames, Jessie Daniel, 56
Anderson, Ada C., 70, 71, 94, 102,
    103
Anderson, Clara, 5
Anderson, Mary Brigham August,
    65
Anderson, Millie, 54–55
Angelou, Maya, 98
Anti-Lynching Crusaders, 56
Archer, Muriel, 103
Army Nurse Corps, 76
Association of Southern Women
    against Lynching, 56

Barnett, Etta Moten, 100–101
Becnel, Nia Dorian, 109
Bird, Charity, 11
Bowden, Artemisia, 35

Branch, Mary Elizabeth, 35, 36
Breed, Henry C., 8
Bright, Geraldine, 76
Briscoe, Hattie, 90–91
Brown, Nellie, 65
Brown, Olive Durden, 31–32

Calloway, Jane, 23
Carr, Mariah, 2
Carrier, Naomi, 107
Carter, Jimmy, 115, 116
Carwin, Joyce Yerwood, 62, 64
Chandler, Mable M., 93
Chisum, Ethelyn Taylor, 31, 32, 34
Civil Rights Act, 114, 136
Civil rights movement, 82–94
Clark, Douglas Mae Campbell, 31
Clinton, Bill, 146
Coleman, Bessie, 60–62
Community Welfare Association,
    42
Conley, Karyne Jones, 24–25
Conner, Jeffie O. A., 66
Connor, Connie Yerwood, 62–63
Conrad, Barbara, 101–102
Cosby, Bill, 104

Covington, Jessie (Dent), 100
Covington, Mrs. B. J., 56–57, 100
Craft, Juanita, 86–88
Craven, Judith L., 64
Crow, Jim, 48–49
Cuney, Adelina Dowdie, 20–22
Cuney, Adeline, 20, 22
Cuney, Maud (Hare), 21, 22–23
Cuney, Norris Wright, 20, 22

Dallas Progressive Voters League, 57
Darling, Katie, 6, 18
Davis, Clarissa, 109
Delco, Exalton, 120
Delco, Wilhelmina, 119–121
Delta Sigma Theta, 39, 108
Dent, Jessie Covington, 100
De Zavala, Mrs. Lorenzo, 12
Dodd, Frederica Chase, 39–41
Douglass, Frederick, 38
Douglass Club, 38, 39, 40
Dowdie, Adelina (Cuney), 20
Dupree, Anna, 42
Dupree, Clarence, 42
Durden, Mattie E., 31

Edelen, Loretta, 120
Eisenhower, Dwight D., 125
Eliza, a slave, 7
Elliott, William, 149
Ewell, Sallie, 34
Ewell, Yvonne, 60

Fanuel, Christine, 103
Farmer-Patrick, Sandra, 109
Fitzgerald-Brown, Benita, 109
Flanagan, Minnie, 57
Floyd, Francine Frazier, 68, 69
Freedmen's Bureau, 54
Freeman, Ruth L., 76
Fuller, Maud A. B., 44
Fuller, William Handy, 44

Garrison, Zina, 110
George, Zelma Watson, 55, 125–126
Gershwin, George, 100
Gibson, Mary Anne, 28
Girl Scouts of the U.S.A., 44–45
Granger, Gen. Gordon, 18
Green, Leola, 76
Guidry, Carlette, 111, 112
Gunter, Alma, 97–98

Hardin, Samuel H., 11
Harding, Warren G., 53
Hare, Maud Cuney, 21, 22–23
Houston, Sam, 12
Humphery, Gladys, 79
Hunt, Annie Mae, 15, 107
Huston-Tillotson College, 32.
    See also Samuel Huston
    College; Tillotson College

International Ladies' Garment
    Workers Union (ILGWU), 79–80

Jacket, Barbara Jean, 111–112
Jemison, Mae C., 71–72
Jim Crow, 48–49
Johnson, Eddie Bernice, 115–117,
    124
Johnson, Iola, 68
Johnson, Lyndon B., 134, 139
Jones, Alice Marie, 76
Jones, Mrs. E. G., 65
Jones, Mrs. J. A., 42–43
Jones, Sadie, 40
Jordan, Arlyne Patten, 129, 135
Jordan, Barbara Charline, vii, 1, 13,
    25, 37, 47, 59, 73, 81, 92, 96, 114,
    115, 127–151
Jordan, Benjamin, 129, 135, 138
Jordan, Bennie, 129, 130
Jordan, Rose Mary, 129, 130

Kennedy, John F., 134
King, Alice Taylor, 67
King, Charles B., 67
King, Martin Luther, Jr., 69
Ku Klux Klan, 54, 55, 56, 122

LEAP (Leadership Educational
    Arts Program), 71, 102–103
Lee, Sheila Jackson, 117–119
Lewis, Marguerite (Mae Dee), 108
Lewis, Mary Elizabeth, 40
Lincoln, Abraham, 18
Long, Jane, 8
Long, Kian, 8

Louis, Joe, 67
Lundy, Anne, 102
Lynchings, 53–54
Lynn, Barbara, 101

McDaniel, Myra, 123
McDonald, Gabrielle, 121–123
McFarland, Fanny, 11
McKnight, Mamie L., 41
Malone-Mayes, Vivienne, 82
Martin, Louise, 68–69
Matthews, Maggie, 28
Mays, Osceola, 100
Means, Bertha S., 94
Merritt, Susan, 26
Miller, Mintie Maria, 7, 16
Morgan, Emily (West), 12
Morgan, Tamar, 11
Morton, Azie Taylor, 115
Mothers Action Council, 94
Mullins, Hannah, 6, 54

NAACP (National Association
    for the Advancement of
    Colored People), 82, 84,
    85–87, 121
Nail Club, 43
National Council of Negro
    Women, 117
National Negro Health League, 41
National Women's Conference,
    45–46
Nixon, Richard M., 140–141, 142

Patten, John Ed, 128–129
Patten, Thelma, 128
Pierce, Aaronetta, 98–99
Pierce, Joseph A., Jr., 98
Polk, Naomi, 96–97
Poll tax, 52–53
Prairie View (originally Prairie
    View State Normal and
    Industrial Institute, now
    Prairie View A&M University),
    33–35, 67, 76, 77, 78, 92, 111, 131

Rachel, a free woman of color, 54
Randon, Matilda Boozie, 65
Ransom, Ethel, 56
Rashad, Phylicia, 104–105, 106
Rawlston, Olivia, 79–80
Rhodie, a slave, 7
Richards, Ann, 121, 145, 151
Richardson, Thelma Paige, 30
Robinson, Dorothy Redus, 29–30,
    83–85
Robinson, Frank, 84
Rowan, Mrs. I. W., 58
Rydolph, Gertrude Ross, 23, 24

Sampson, Edith, 131
Samuel Huston College, 32, 33, 108
Santa Anna, Gen. Antonio
    López de, 12
Scales, Clara, 28
Scott, Gloria, 44–46

Shaw, Isabella, 28
Shelton, Issie, 133
Simmons, Kitty, 49, 51
Simmons, Ruth, 69–70
Simond, Ada DeBlanc, 108
Smith, Lucille Bishop, 67
Surles, Carol, 36
Sweatt v. Painter, 35, 132
Swoopes, Sheryl, 110–111

Taylor, Mary Ellen, 55
Texas Commission on Inter-racial
    Cooperation, 56–57
Texas Southern University
    (formerly Texas State
    University for Negroes), 35, 92,
    131–133
Texas Woman's University, 36
Thompson, Mary Yerwood, 40
Thompson, Senfronia, 124
Tillotson College, 31, 32, 33, 35
Truman, Harry S., 76

United Packing House Workers of
    America, 79

Voting rights, 49–53, 136

Warren, Mary A., 23
West, Emily (Morgan), 12
White, Hattie Mae (Mrs. Charles
    E.), 89–90

White, Lulu B., 85
White, Mark, 123
White, Mattie B. (Mrs. Thomas J.), 24
Williams, Augustine, 67
Williams, Elizabeth "Tex," 74, 75
Women's Army Corps (WAC), 74–75, 76
Woods, Stephanie, 109
Wright, Annie Lois Brown, 76

Yellow Rose of Texas, 12
Yerwood, Charles, 62
Yerwood, Connie (Connor), 62–63
Yerwood, Joyce (Carwin), 62, 64
Young, Andrew, 124
YWCA, 41